TO A YOUNG JAZZ MUSICIAN

MAY 2021

Congratulations on
all your accomplishments!
－Emily Black

RANDOM HOUSE TRADE PAPERBACKS | NEW YORK

Wynton Marsalis

TO A YOUNG
JAZZ MUSICIAN

LETTERS FROM THE ROAD

WITH Selwyn Seyfu Hinds

Published in the United States by Random
House Trade Paperbacks, an imprint of The
Random House Publishing Group, a division
of Random House, Inc., New York.

RANDOM HOUSE TRADE PAPERBACKS and
colophon are registered trademarks of
Random House, Inc.

Originally published in hardcover in the
United States by Random House, an imprint
of The Random House Publishing Group,
a division of Random House, Inc., in 2004.

ISBN 0-8129-7420-4

Printed in the United States of America

www.atrandom.com

20 19 18 17 16

To all the parents who take their kids to concerts

that they don't necessarily like and then wait for the kids

to get autographs, lessons, and whatever else.

When you set out to make a dramatic statement—make it.

Deal with the fallout later.

ACKNOWLEDGMENTS

Ricki Moskowitz

CONTENTS

*Don't run away from your issues. Take that glance in
the mirror that crumples all your hardened certainties
about the world. Everyone wants his or her own truth
to be the only truth. Jazz music's power comes from
its ability to take you deeper into yourself, to a
relationship within. I want you to go past the
arrogance of your position into a love of the sound of
the music. And pursue your version of that intangible,
consistent beauty you hear in the greats.*

*Why do they run from the truth in this music? The
strange dialogue of race, jazz, and America. Our
culture has experienced a decline of intellectual rigor
along with an unchecked decadence. When there's a
greater degree of decadence, a higher level of heroism
is required to combat it because there's much less
reward.*

*What happens when whatever integrity you hold fast
to runs up against the lack of integrity in the culture
in which you have to define yourself? Pandering to
the marketplace or the academy is commonplace
because it leads to clear rewards. But corruption*

*certainly creeps in when you pander to your own
deficiencies: You can't play fast, so no one should
play fast. You can't play slow, so ballads are not
worth playing. You can't play on changes, so changes
are outmoded. You can't play a freer, fluid form of
expression, so no one else should. I suppose the central
issue comes down to the fact that we don't have a
conception of morality in music.*

The First Movement

Phone conversation is one thing; a letter lasts. I love the intimacy of letters, the warm communication that flows between two people who take the time to write. It reminds me of dialogue on the bandstand. What better way to talk to a young jazz musician? Words frozen on paper like a recording. I think about all the lessons I've had with some of the greatest musicians: Art Blakey, Dizzy, Sweets, John Lewis, Gerry Mulligan, Sarah Vaughan, Danny Barker. I recall the wonderful nurturing conversations with so many phenomenal people now gone from this world: Sir Roland Hanna, Miles, Ray Brown—oh man!, so many. I've heard lots of stories and received great, firsthand instruction from them. Invaluable nuggets, man. Many deep words, some made thin by time and the fallibility of memory. I wish I had some letters from them.

As I travel around the country, around the world, I always meet groups of people who love to talk about issues and respond to my experiences. And I've long wanted to set some of those ideas, and the thoughts inspired by those responses, in the kind of book that can answer many of the concerns of younger musicians. Whatever parts of the globe they may come from, these young people are bonded by a search for meaning. You might think they're mainly interested in technical information, but that sort of information is abundantly available. Mostly they seek meaning from me. They want to know: Who did you know? What did they say? What was it like playing with Art Blakey? Is it all right to be me? See, that's the main thing younger people want to know—is it okay to be themselves, as musicians, as human beings?

In my teaching I try to give some answers: "Of course it's all right to be you. And not only is it all right to be you, you are your greatest creation." I try to convey my sense of jazz as well, my understanding of its direction and meaning. When you play with musicians, when you just talk with people, you realize that each person has a direction in life. Specific ideas that he or she thinks and believes and feels. An art form is no different from life. The objectives are broader, of course, because an art form includes all of us—our aspirations, our memories, our contrary ways of thinking.

That's why the deeper you go into an art, the more you learn about yourself and about living. Art interprets mythology, and jazz interprets American mythology. Jazz speaks to a certain truth of the soul of our nation. And it will speak to the truth of your soul as a human being. When you contemplate the wisdom in jazz, eventually you see the objectives of the music as your objectives. Then you realize that the objectives of your music align with the proclaimed objectives of your nation: To improvise means to invent your own way of intelligently using what you have in order to improve your environment; to swing means to maintain equilibrium with elegance, to be resilient; and to play the blues means that no matter how tragic a situation may be, you have the capacity to conquer it with style. The blues recognizes the importance of human will: It says, "I'm down now. But I can always get up." Not, "I'm down now. I might as well stay down." If it did that, it wouldn't be "the blues." It would just be "blues." The "get up" part is what makes it "the blues."

Later.

TO A YOUNG JAZZ MUSICIAN

The Humble Self

June 4, 2003

Dear Anthony,

Today would have been a good day for you to hang with us. We just pulled into Maine for a performance. Did the usual bit: check in at the hotel, head to the venue for sound check, back to the hotel to change for the show. Oh, and look for lobster. I also had a chance to talk to some kids about playing. They were high school age, a bit younger than you. People filled the school auditorium—dads, moms, brothers and sisters, cousins. All watched the kids in the school's jazz band. Those kids did well. It touched me to hear them play so earnestly, to watch them listen so intently in their effort to get better. And I love the feeling of pride and expectation that pours out of families as they enjoy the results of hard work on display. You should have seen the drummer; fifteen years old. Trying to be so cool we called him Ice. He looked great, but damn sure wasn't swinging. Afterward, I ended up telling 'em the usual: stay encouraged, play with each other, and keep practicing. I wonder sometimes if saying "practice" is enough. Practice what? Talking with those kids brought to mind something someone once asked John Coltrane, "Trane, when do you practice?"

"I only practice when I'm working on something," he replied.

Yeah, man, you can play tunes forever. Play enough, play every night, and you'll get to blow on a lot of songs. Cats with experience get to know the changes and play lots of different tunes. But you, and those kids in Maine, don't have Coltrane's experience. So practice means practice the "something" Trane talked about. It could be your sound, a deeper swing, solo construction, or just hearing bass lines. The bottom line is practice "something" every moment you can. Don't just sit around and wait for something to happen; that same something is waiting on you.

I spent time thinking about what we should talk about in this first letter, and I came to the notion of humility. You consider yourself humble? Ever really think about it? Let me tell you, humility is the doorway to truth and clarity of objectives for a jazz musician; it's the doorway to learning. Check it out.

When you start playing, you've got to have objectives: What are you playing? Why are you playing it? How do you want to sound, and how will you achieve that sound? When you have those things clear in your mind, it's much easier to teach yourself, and ultimately, that's what you have to do. No one will teach you how to play.

I've been lucky: Early on in my career I spent a good deal of time around great musicians, Art Blakey, for instance. You might ask me, "What did Art Blakey teach you?" And I'd tell you "nothing," at least in the way you probably meant the question. Art didn't say "play your scales" or "play a G on this." You'd start playing, and he would tell you something like, "You need to be more physical." Or he would come in and say, "You're bullshitting." That was your lesson. What did that mean? Stop bullshitting. That's Art. That's what he taught you. You watched him and he played with maximum intensity all the time.

Today you have more and more jazz musicians graduating from universities. But many of these institutions overemphasize playing scales, patterns, and spelling out harmonies. How many times have you heard of an older cat grumbling that these young kids can't play nothing but fast nothing? That leaves some to question the value of institutional training in jazz when they should be questioning the values of the institutions. Kids are being miseducated into believing that fulfilling a few technical objectives is actually playing. Style over substance. Like a lot of academic writing, piles of big words around small ideas that add up to one response: "Huh?"

If you wanted to study engineering, certain basic, fundamental levels of technical expertise would just be assumed when you showed up for college. At Jazz U., the meaningless spools of scales, chords, and fast runs that are belabored ad infinitum don't form a curriculum of advanced study. These techniques will not take you where you need to go to develop musicianship and personal direction. They won't develop your conception, nor unleash your personal power.

In fact, it's a question relevant to just about any situation in which you find yourself: How do I unleash my personal power? Most relationships will require you to address the issue of how you participate as yourself without being selfish. And in jazz, personal power is your unique creativity. When you codify, articulate, and project your own hard-earned objectives through an instrument, you unleash *your* personal power.

Let's say you learn a piece in class, and you play it again and again—eight thousand times. You'll be so tired of doing it that every time you gotta do it again, you'll say to yourself, "Man, not this!" And if it's part of a course of study in school, maybe you've done it for two or three years now. It could be twenty-five years. You can repeat something forever or you can look for things. "Things" are possibilities, and possibilities never run out. That's why the music lives on. Consider the rhythm section alone. They can slow down. They can speed up. They can be solo-specific and change grooves. And you, playing with them, you realize the different things you could do on your own. You can interact with your drummer. You could modulate to another key. You could do a million things with it.

Or you can do nothing with it and twenty-five years from now, you will go all over the world and play with people who play the same basic form that has been played since the late 1940s. Melody, a string of too long solos, then you'll play a long one (even though you know better), then a bass solo. Everyone will play his or her own version of the common vocabulary. So start now, don't accept this for yourself. Unleash the unlimited freedom in the music for your unique articulation. Don't just stand up and play clichés all the time, all night, the same patterns. Use your ingenuity and your creativity.

To do this, you must develop some objectives. When you have objectives, when you understand what you're trying to do, then you're free to try things when you play. They might sound sad at first, but you have an idea—you're working those things out. It's important to realize that in order to be different, you have to do something different. The first inkling of difference comes with thinking a different way. Then, make sure that that thinking reflects how you truly feel.

Let's rap about your favorite musician for a second, Charlie Parker. Whenever Charlie Parker used to play Jazz at the Philharmonic with other all-star musicians, they would always play these obnoxious riffs behind him. He didn't like it, but they did it anyway. Why? Maybe, unconsciously, the others didn't want to hear Parker's playing because it stoked a kind of anxious competitiveness in them. They didn't want to deal with the weight and power of what he played. They weren't purposefully thinking, "He's playing great, let's cut him off with this riff." Maybe it was the psychological impact of being on the bandstand with a musician of real genius.

Parker had specific components in his art: Midwestern root music; the Kansas City blues; and a fleet-footed conception of melodic virtuosity, absolute technical clarity; and a way of playing the shuffle rhythm in a manner distinct from Lester Young. Bird was a great musician and he had a different mind for music, but the bottom line on the vocabulary and the objectives was clear. That's why so much of Charlie Parker's early material is the blues, the American popular song, and originals that have that song form.

But at a certain point, all of that foundation work became unimportant to his acolytes. How can I explain? Well, when somebody puts on a two-thousand-dollar suit, you tend to look at the suit and not the person. Charlie Parker's surface style was fast, and it had a certain type of flash to it. Underneath, the soulful melodies, the blues, that Midwestern swing, and other earthy elements required to successfully carry that level of sophistication were not as apparent. You see, the flash blinded you.

When root objectives are lost, it becomes impossible to give birth to new things. The best that you can hope for is to create another form with an entirely different meaning. The proof sits before us. For all the talk of innovation, we don't hear as much as we should, given the mountains of talents out here. We need jazz youth to go deeper into the American soil, where all the minerals and nutrients congregate. People are not being moved the way Parker or Armstrong or Erroll Garner moved them. The late, great composer John Lewis once told me he would go to hear Charlie Parker and there would be all types of people listening: longshoremen, policemen, people who simply heard his sound and were touched by it. Lewis would be hurrying home and just happen to stop in a club for a second, but Charlie Parker's playing was so gripping it made him stay.

When we teach Charlie Parker, that's what we should focus on. What gave him this relationship to his environment? What gave his playing such power? You need to evoke that or some portion of it to get a good grade. The flashy style can come later. After Parker there came a point where style was elevated over substance, conventions over objectives. Don't confuse conventions with the objectives of the form. For example, after Charlie Parker, everybody started trying to play his melodies on their instruments. Trombone players started playing like Charlie Parker; bass players wanted to play Charlie Parker; piano players wanted to play Charlie Parker. Granted, a lot of piano players sounded great in that style, but one of the strongest advantages of the piano is the capacity to voice separate melodies simultaneously when playing with two hands. Now, because Charlie Parker played with a single-voice instrument, no pianists are gonna stride with two hands? Or take the three-horn New Orleans counterpoint. 'Cause Bird didn't do it, was it no longer worth doing? Or not modern? You see, that's the problem with following a part of something as if it's the whole thing. Who are you: a part of a fad, or a jazz musician?

As you grow older, self-knowledge becomes one of the hardest things to acquire. In our context, as jazz musicians, it's more difficult than you think—to know what you will play; how your playing will evolve; how to play with others. Much like those cats playing with Bird, quick to riff. Something said, "Get in Bird's way." Thus, "Mess the music up." The first level of mastery occurs over self. And the first test of mastery over one's self is humility. True humility. You look at yourself and say, "Man, I don't want to be sad anymore. I want to learn how to play." Humility has nothing to do with me, your friends, your lady; and it's in such short supply out here, man.

Do you know how you can tell when someone is truly humble? I believe there's one simple test: because they consistently observe and listen, the humble improve. They don't assume, "I know the way." Of the hundreds, perhaps thousands, of musicians that I've worked with, I've seen true, continuous development in eight or nine. That's in twenty, twenty-five years, man. In most of my experiences with musicians, I hear them when they're fifteen or so and I think, "Damn, this guy's unbelievable." Then all the obstacles of life appear, and by the time they're twenty-five or twenty-six, I think, "How did that happen? How did you start with this much ability, this much genius, and this much creativity, and end up here ten years later?" Man, it's hard out here.

Understand something, Anthony: You will hear the same thing over and over again, but you have to develop the requisite humility to learn, to love to learn. Humility engenders learning because it beats back the arrogance that puts blinders on. It leaves you open for truths to reveal themselves. You don't stand in your own way. You realize: It's all about you. Your learning won't live or die with your school or me. You have to become the center of your education. Once you accept that, you'll understand that learning means figuring out what you need to do to get where you want to be. I hope I'm not beating the point to death, but I have to make you understand the importance of your personal involvement in your own growth and development.

Some people don't show up for class. In truth, they don't want to go to school. But that has nothing to do with any teacher. It's your own time and opportunity lost. What if the commitment was a job? You might have been told to show up at 9:00 A.M., or hand in paperwork by Friday. And you don't. So they fire you. Your employer is not going to have much interest in asking, "Why didn't you show up on time?" That's for your parents, or people who love you with such intensity that they feel a sense of personal loss when you bullshit.

Real life won't work that way. A jazz musician's life won't work that way. People don't know, or care, about your issues. They spend hard-earned money to go out and enjoy some music that they want to hear. So it's incumbent upon you to figure out: "What do I want to do? Will it kill me to learn how to play this difficult music and develop my voice so that I can play something provocative enough for people to want to spend their time listening to me? What do I have that I can present to people that will make them feel better about being alive?"

This is a tough thing we do, a tough road we travel. It demands your respect and commitment; it lives through your humility. Man, listen: Whether you're a grizzled veteran, a nineteen-year-old like yourself, or in high school like those kids back in Maine, as jazz musicians we're engaged in the same thing—grown folks' business. So treat it seriously, man. 'Cause it damn sure will treat you seriously.

In the spirit of swing.

2

A Human Thing

June 18, 2003

Dear Anthony,

I've got a lot on my mind that needs passing to you. Today, I'd like to cover a good bit of ground: more lessons inherent in the great Charlie Parker, some tales from my own musician's road, and some thoughts about the three P words—patience, persistence, and productivity. Man, you'll need to hold on to all three of those words to play jazz well—not to mention writing letters. So don't get worked up if the pace of my writing is slower than your own. I promise to get to these letters when I can, jot a few lines to you during those gaps between the bus ride, the sound check, and the gig. Yeah, I realize you want to taste this life for yourself. May as well show you some of the things you need to know. We'll keep this simple—just a few thoughts back and forth between you and me. And it won't be all formal and overbearing, because that's not how jazz is made. I'll just pass you some thoughts on life and music, because, ultimately, they end up as one and the same. By the way, you wanted to know about coming to see me at my place in New York when you get here—no problem, man. My house is always filled with people. We'll just hook things up when I get back to town. And don't call; just drop by. Otherwise you'll never catch me.

So let's rap about these P words a bit, patience first of all. Patience will enter in through many doors: You need patience with the arc of your own development, and you need patience with your fellow musicians, many of whom will be less than serious. You need patience with critics. With friends who are uninterested in any art. See, in jazz you need other people. You can't be as self-involved and narcissistic as you want to be, because jazz *is* your musical interaction with others.

And persistence? You need persistence because playing jazz is a life replete with self-doubt and difficulties that never go away—they just change. Once you get on this road, you gonna be on it. It won't get easier. It doesn't matter if your popularity grows, or if you make money. More money and popularity won't matter, because the act of creation and remaining invigorated to create can't be purchased or hyped. Gravity never stops pushing. Persistence helps you push back.

And you have to be productive: What you do is what you will do. I had a friend I played football with back in Kenner, Louisiana. Before a game we would all be in the car braggin' and talkin' about what we were gonna do. But this friend would wait until you messed something up: You dropped a pass, got a flag thrown on you, missed an interception or a tackle, you cost the team something. Then he would walk down the bench real slow, bend down into your face mask, and he would scream as loud as he could, "Let's see, motherfucker, let's see!" We'd laugh, 'cause it would break the tension after you'd messed up. But it also let you know that you had to get back up and redeem yourself: Let's see now; let's see what you're made of. That's always in your life, man. Whether you drop a football, mess up your solo, or initiate a bad relationship. How will you get up? "Let's see!" Continue to produce no matter what.

Coming to New York to become a jazz musician you'd better be prepared to drop a few footballs. Man, I remember when I came up. Word had spread: "There's a cat from New Orleans that can play. He's gonna come up here and he's gonna be playin' jazz." I went to a jam session up in Harlem at the Red Rooster with a trumpeter named Bucky Thorpe; he was still alive back then. And Tom Browne was at this jam session. Now, Tom Browne had put out a hit called "Funkin' for Jamaica." I'm thinking, "They don't have no integrity, man. He plays trumpet for a hobby. He's out here piloting airplanes and shit. I'm hungry. I'm up here to straighten all this shit out." And the cats, the older guys, would say that, too. I was seventeen at the time.

So I walk into the club, and the guys say, "Yeah, there's that cat from New Orleans! He gonna straighten this shit out. Yeah, go jump on Tom Browne." So I pulled my horn out. And man, he cut a huge gaping hole in my ass, just tore me up that night. Then he looked at me as if to say, "You the kid that's supposed to be straightening this shit out?" And one of the older cats who had just boosted me up before I got on the bandstand shook his head and said, "Man, if you what they sending up here, Lord help us."

But that was a good experience because that let me know that it's not about what you think, or what it appears to be. It's about what *is*. And what it was right then was Tom Browne's foot in my behind. Now with all that "Funkin' for Jamaica" and whatever condescending thoughts I had about funk music, once we started playing, he outplayed me. That was a wake-up call.

Another time I sat in with Mel Lewis's band. And it was the same murmuring: "Yeah, this boy here from New Orleans who can play." He made me wait until the last tune. And then he called out a tune in D-flat minor, a shuffle. I had never played in the key of D-flat minor. I didn't know the tune. It showed. I sounded thoroughly sad.

Afterward, nobody told me nothin'. Cats packed up their horns. Lewis just shook his head, like, "Oh man, you've got to be joking!" That was the message that was communicated to me: I'm too sad to be up here in New York. I got so depressed, because you tend to see everything you do as life's crucial moment. "Ain't been in town one month and already I got my head cut. I went to sit in with this man, and now he ain't even lookin' at me." And I'm coming from New Orleans, where I'm being celebrated. Man, I wanted to go home. But then I thought about my homeboy: "Let's see, mothafucka." You know, even now at forty-one, I still think about him in those types of moments. So, I got up the next morning and started dealing with D-flat minor.

Our conversation before the tour got me thinking about roads. This road—and this tour bus—that I'll be on for the next few weeks, and the road you're walking down as you learn this art form. You seem so compelled to figure it out. Man, you sure packed enough questions into your first letter. Hey, that curiosity will work for you, but guard against it driving you to frustration. Answers won't always pop up, because when you learn music, you have to understand context in order to make sense of many things. You're always seeking meaning and form. Why is this here? What purpose does that serve? Ultimately, you want your playing to be purposeful. And those things that sound random, you want them to be random by design. You don't want that to be a case of "Oops! That's not what I meant. I hope it will come out okay." Mastery is never a matter of not knowing. If it were, there would be more people lucking up into it. And you wouldn't need to seek information.

You've told me of your love and reverence for Charlie Parker's music. Now, Charlie Parker was a genius of the first order. For all his personal problems, he had timeless insights into what it means to be alive. And he also set standards of technical excellence, a quickness of thought and depth of expression that will always challenge you. Here's the beautiful thing: As you grow as a musician, your understanding of him will deepen. And the way you hear his playing will deepen, as well. You'll love him even more.

I'll tell you the main lesson in Parker's playing: Have confidence in how you feel about things. See, Parker played Charlie Parker, not bebop. People say he played bebop, but he played himself. As a musician you have to believe in your own expression, and you can't look around for the answer. How would anyone else know? That's the underlying lesson of Charlie Parker's music: Be yourself. Duke Ellington said it best: "It's better to be a number one yourself than a number two somebody else." The paradox with listening to someone like Bird is that his personality is so strong it pulls you in his direction. But you earn your individuality by encountering these strong personalities and still deciding on your own way.

When you listen to the greatest musicians, someone like Charlie Parker, don't merely listen to the notes they play or the harmonic content. The notes are merely the covering, the façade. Listen to what they express. Then you will hear meaning. And that meaning, that reality, is far more important than the notes or the harmony, because the notes of the harmony are obvious and finite. You have to search for the meaning and there are infinite implications in each nuance. Over the next few weeks, I'll talk about one of the great misconceptions in our music—the supposed battle between technical proficiency and emotional reality. In fact, you're probably gonna get tired of me harping on it. But much as I may urge the connection with emotion and feeling, keep in mind: Emotion and feeling don't make up the whole story, because if you can't play the notes and the harmony, you're not going to be like Parker and the rest. You'll just be inept.

Some folks are fortunate enough to be melodic wellsprings. Charlie Parker, of course, was surrounded by melodies, root melodies: church music, Kansas City blues, country blues, American popular song. He liked a lot of music, all kinds of melodic songs. They were a part of the fabric of his everyday life. That was his age. You don't live in that type of age. So you have to function like a griot or musicologist like Béla Bartók. You have to carry the melodic meaning of your culture with you. Sometimes an artist is born into a golden age. Then he or she can state the ideas already transpiring with greater clarity. In other ages, he may have to counterstate the trends, to bring things back, or to redirect them. We can't control what age we're born in. But responses and meaningful statements can be made in any age.

As you listen to Charlie Parker and any of the great melodic jazz players, you'll wonder: Where will I get my melodies? Where will they come from? If you can't figure out where your melodies come from then you'll be reduced to playing scales on chords, and that will never produce good music. Unfortunately, you're learning in an age that's neither melodic nor romantic. So you've got to figure out where to go to get stuff if you want certain elements in your music. Search. Like when you hear a word whose meaning you don't know, you go look it up. What if you hear a phrase played by Charlie Parker and you don't know what it means? Well, you're probably not going to know you don't know what it means. In all likelihood, you won't have any idea that you don't know, because you will be the only one among your friends who's trying to play. Well, don't ask them. Try to find someone who knows. A visiting jazz musician or the local true jazz aficionado. Don't ever be discouraged. Search.

As a teen, I never heard any of my friends, those who were not musicians themselves, say the *name* of any jazz musician. Ever. Over seventeen years, of all the guys I grew up with, playing ball and everything else, I never heard any of them say the name of any jazz artist in any context. No Louis Armstrong. No Miles Davis. No Charlie Parker. I'm not talking preference. I'm not saying that someone might have said, "I don't like John Coltrane." They'd never heard of him. I never looked down on anyone for that; the only reason I knew about jazz was because my daddy played.

Musical and cultural development ebbed when my generation came up, and what had happened before wasn't transferred to us. We mainly played pop and funk music. The church music was slowly being corrupted and a lot of the great jazz legends had sold out. We didn't have the type of national leadership we needed. Some of the more popular ones still hung on, like Art Blakey; but we thought them old. Certain younger artists still played—Woody Shaw, for instance. But older jazz musicians, in the main, focused on the effort to get a hit. Forget transferring information.

For us youngsters, if you liked music, if you could even tell the difference between real jazz and funk, the question was,

"Why play jazz?" You didn't feel meaning—girls didn't like it; no one made money from it. When I was a kid, we equated the past with degradation and the useless. We didn't learn that the past held anything other than segregation. Sure, you could have taken my father's jazz class, but there were probably five of us in there. And, frankly, we didn't know what he was talking about, because none of the values he espoused through the music resonated with anything else in our lives. We knew about *Super Fly*, we knew about James Brown, we knew about Stevie Wonder, we knew about Kool and the Gang. We knew what it took to get your ass whipped. We knew who cooked the best gumbo, who had the best pool game, who played the best ball, and who was fast.

Under those conditions it's difficult to piece together a philosophy strong enough to sustain an artistic impulse. Even if you had the impulse, you had to put your salesman's shoes on; you had to persuade everyone else to try to play something they didn't believe in.

Man, back then it would have been nice had I known some of the things I know now, though I suppose we all say that. I wish I had known the importance of going to the sources for information. That's simple enough, right? Don't rely on the old adage "Everyone knows." Want to learn about Scott Joplin? Go to his manuscripts. Jelly Roll Morton? Check out his tapes. What Duke Ellington had to say about a subject?

The answers sit right in his interviews. And I would have spoken to the older musicians in more detail. As a teen I didn't have the understanding or context to know what they were talking about. I'd rap with cats like Roy Eldridge and Sweets Edison. But the essence of what they said slipped by me. I understood some; but had I known the significance of what they had done, I would have pursued their knowledge with much more fervor.

I just kept searching on my own, kept trying to get better, kept trying to understand my one thing. And as you follow this road, Anthony, it will keep leading you back to that, because you have only one thing to interpret. That one thing may have many ways to it, many facets. But it's one thing all the same: what you understand, what you can do. If you can do it, you can do it. If you can't do it, you can't. Don't take that negatively. Since there's only the one thing, and there are many ways of doing that one thing, folks have the capacity to do it. Thing is, most don't want to. Because doing the one thing means sacrifice. All too often you have many *it*s that you want to pursue, and sometimes they conflict, a tussle right there on the boundary among three great *do*s: what you *can do*, what you *should do*, and what you *want to do*. When the three sit aligned, you're all right. But usually they fight. It's up to you to bring the *do*s together. This is where patience, persistence, and productivity reenter.

Now, it's not easy. Too often what you *want to do* is not what you *should do;* sometimes what you *should do* is not what you *can do.* And sometimes what you *can do* is not what you *want to do.* With me, I always wanted to play. I always wanted to play, in spite of what anyone else did. Well, once I got serious about playing, at any rate. I wanted to be in that certain place where the older cats would respect me. Real respect, not the lip service that became customary because they had given up on the younger musicians, given up to the point that everything you played they would applaud: "Man, it's great. We just glad to see somebody *trying* to play."

A sense of integrity guided me. I wanted to hear myself playing in that certain place and I knew I wasn't there. That drove my search. See, mentorship was a strange thing for me in those days. It gave me both great and little influence in my own development: great influence in terms of knowing what *had happened;* very little influence in terms of what *needed to happen.* Because of the great changes in the civil rights movement and the rock revolution, most of the mentors understood what they knew from their time, but they couldn't understand our time. I suppose that's a lot to ask of someone.

Things have changed today. For one, a lot more people can play now. More people are invested and interested in playing now than when I came up. On trumpet alone you've got Ryan Kisor, Marcus Printup, Jeremy Pelt, Mike Rodriguez, and Jean Jones. Piano players like Danilo Pérez, Aaron Gold-berg, Eric Reed, and Eric Lewis. That reality can't help but keep you optimistic about the state of the art form. Though, to be honest, man, I have no problem mustering optimism. Jazz itself is so great, it will produce people that can play. Art forms exist across time because the greatest people with the most talent are driven to them. Why? Great art issues challenges. And artists love to be tested. As long as people play saxophone, they will be challenged by Charlie Parker. And with art, people speak to one another's cultures across time. Sixteenth-century counterpoint could be revived if someone could make it live. Like Shakespeare revived the tragedy. Like Picasso revived so many forms. It simply comes down to who makes a decision to take on the challenge, regardless of era.

The level of playing today may not stack up to past eras, because players, generally speaking, don't possess the same degree of consciousness. And there's less pressure. If people put a lot of pressure on you, man, you're going to play better. There was a time when the use of the word "no" carried power in a jam session; not like today's mutual admiration societies. But that, too, is subject to time. That attitude could reverse, because the performances produced on those classic records will always be around for people to listen to, to know what great jazz playing sounds like. You have to know where the standard lies.

I love this music, man. It pushes me, artistically, personally. I got to hear it. But it's deeper than the music. For me, it's
about people. It's about a thing, a human thing, the best of
what comes out of us—a consciousness, a feeling, a way.
That's why I enjoy listening to people play live more than any
CD; but don't believe that it's not possible for contemporary
practitioners to reach or transcend those moments of greatness
frozen on classic CDs. We can and sometimes do. There was a
time when I wondered. Now I know. People are still playing.
It doesn't make a difference whether someone else is enam-
ored with what was. The road leads back to you. Whether *you*
can hear it or not, and do *you* go out to hear people play. Listening is a part of practice. I see Frank Wess out listening to
people all the time. Dressed down at eighty-something and
still swinging.

I used to hear my daddy and them talk about going to the
woodshed. Man, I thought the woodshed was a place where
you got your behind whipped. And it is, but it's also the place
where you get your stuff together. You know, Charlie Parker
got a cymbal thrown at him; he went into the woodshed and
came out with a technique to play the music he needed to play.
And we still need to go there. That's why we call practice
"shedding." By the way, practice—there's another P word for
you.

That reminds me: Don't forget that productivity. You want to be a musician? Get out and play gigs. Remember the simple equation: What you do is what you will do. So if you play, you will play. If you bullshit, well, that too will speak for itself, right?

Keep being Anthony.

3

Talking Rules,
Singing Freedom

July 2, 2003

Dear Anthony,

I've been playing chess with my sons since they were
seven and eight years old. But now they got teenage disease. You must know the ailment: You think you're way
better at something than you really are and you're in a
hurry to demonstrate that fact. So they get whipped a lot.
They hear that word "checkmate" and their eyes widen
with disbelief. Then they fuss, grumble, get irate, and
come back for more. We play a lot of chess on these bus
rides between towns. And if you ride this bus, as my sons
do when I take them on tour, you gotta know the rules of

the game: what they are, how to bend 'em, and how to use 'em to whup up on someone.

By the questions in your last letter, I'd say you're thinking about rules, too. That doesn't surprise me. Man, rules, and thinking about rules, consume almost every student I know. Regulations just wrap y'all up—worried about what you can or can't do. What? You think that's going to give you the magic formula for playing better? Guess again. Still, I suppose we should go ahead and talk about them some, just to give you some peace of mind.

I already hear the first question rolling around in your head: In jazz, are rules good or bad? Sorry, I can't give that one a yes or no answer. Rules can be good or bad. They don't hold inherent value that can be judged. With a few exceptions, like "no inbreeding," they are just codifications of value judgments. For example, you'll often find someone quoting Coltrane as saying, "Damn the rules. It's the feeling that counts." That's a convenient quote—Trane says damn the rules. And it ends up used as a justification for anything. You ask me something about rhythm changes. I say, "Man, you know rhythm changes, why are we talking about that? Damn the rules, it's the feeling that counts." Well, "Damn the rules" ends up being a rule.

I prefer to get you into a realm of thinking that is defined not by answers about rules and regulations, but rather by the process and experience through which you construct your own music and style. Ultimately, the how and why of that process will lead you to the correct consideration, and value, of rules.

Consider three thoughts: First, are the structures of jazz so enslaving that you have to be free from them? Or do they pose a challenge, like the boundaries of a football game, which if discarded make playing less liberating? Second, is it desirous to play for fewer and fewer people? Should you cultivate a superelite because you don't want to maintain any relationship to recognizable forms? Say I choose to discard the rules of English. My need to be original is such that I have to use new words to express myself. So if I want to express "Wonderful, wasn't it?" I say, "Voom a ratoog?" That's okay for me, but what about you? Third, is it possible for you to rebel against a convention of rebellion? Instead of abstracted form, instead of doing things that obliterate form, is it possible for you to be rebellious by creating form? I once had a student for whom this was a regular dialogue. He'd insist, "Well, you know, I'm trying to stretch things out and go to the boundary."

"What boundary are you going out to?" I'd ask.

"Why, I want to be different, I'm developing things and taking them to the outer limits."

"Oh? What outer limit are you taking them to?"

Then he'd go quiet for a spell. That meant he was considering that the outer limit was also a boundary, some place that had to be beyond the inner limit.

In modern American mythology, we're inundated with the notion of the rebel without a cause. You've read it, seen it, and heard it so many times that the philosophy of the disaffected cat just seems natural: trump the world, the hell with it all, let's tear things up. That's the American way. But you want to know the truth? The important part of that slogan is "without a cause." There's scarcely an ounce of rebellion in our minds these days. The Constitution and the Declaration of Independence were acts of rebellion. People risked their lives to express these ideals. What Louis Armstrong played was an act of rebellion. What Duke Ellington wrote was an act of rebellion, and an expression of freedom. But each of those examples created new systems of order and each works in a particular way governed by certain laws and rules.

Freedom lives in structure. Do you think that sounds crazy? Maybe it seems hard to understand: How could there be freedom in a state that you perceive as lacking freedom? Think of these notions of freedom and structure in the context of long-existing forms and practices and ask yourself these questions: Do I have a better way? When I do rebel against the established order, am I truly seeking freedom, or publicity and the comfort of an inept cultish group of some sort? Ask yourself, have I yet to exhaust the possibilities in the forms as they exist? Is the size of what I want to express large enough to require new forms? And, ultimately, what do I want to do with my artistic freedom?

I talk to you about these issues because the road winds back to you and your choices. These are the things I need you to ponder, because the more deeply you think about the problems of your day and the more solutions you propose, the more successful you will be at expressing your identity as an artist.

An old saying seems appropriate here: Never imitate the failures of your nation. Growing up in a particular era can lead you to accept things that society simply presumes to be true. Segregation in this country persisted for years, despite the fact that reasonable and intelligent people knew it to be bankrupt and inhumane. Segregation became reduced to and accepted as custom until enough Americans made the determination to fight perceived custom by saying, "We won't stand for this any longer, so we will go through whatever it takes to effect change." They rebelled and forged a new way that we still work on today.

Profound change can be initiated in any time, even during a self-indulgent era like the one in which we now live, a time when some of the dumbest stuff that you could imagine has become custom. When we played in funk bands in the early seventies, no way in the world could we have imagined the day when someone would come out on a bandstand, grab their johnson, and call themselves derogatory names. You could not have imagined in 1972 that that would be considered entertainment. It would have been inconceivable. But here in 2003 we see it all the time, and it's an expression of certain people's freedom. Now, you're a musician, Anthony. You have the opportunity to exercise your mind, your spirit, your conceptions, and you're going to come into this culture and make some type of statement with your music. You'll expend your freedom in a certain way, likely by creating some type of structure. And those structures may eventually challenge someone else's notion of freedom.

Ask yourself these things as well: What is it in jazz that I find liberating? What do I want to express in jazz? Are the structures of jazz enslaving? And can these structures be liberated through increasing degrees of no structure? Keep in mind that by now the notion of free jazz is almost fifty years old.

Did you know that Coltrane took lessons with Ornette Coleman? Yeah, man, Coltrane paid Coleman for lessons in the early sixties. Coltrane took those lessons so that Coleman could teach him how to break free of harmonic structures. But when you listen to something like "Crescent," "A Love Supreme," or even "Transition," Coltrane still played harmonic progression. Regardless of teaching, Coltrane's method of achieving freedom was not Coleman's.

In our Western way of thinking, true artistic progression in music—not just in jazz—uses abstraction in a proud march toward a state of elitism. Its credo: "The public is not hip enough for this." But should we be striving for an even more elite expression, one that very few people can listen to? Or should we go in the commercial direction, an expression that people can't help but listen to? What objectives do we have? How do we want to express our freedom? Where does our artistic responsibility in this regard lie?

Hey, Anthony, these questions don't come with a right or wrong answer. I just want you to think on them. Never forget, you're on a road, discovering yourself as you go along. Everything we talk about is geared toward making you a better musician. I want to bring you in that direction. I don't want to tell you what to think about music, or give you a conclusion that keeps you from realizing whatever your real potential might be.

Kids come to my classes all the time. Invariably, their teachers have given them some unbending instruction, something they have to do, a way they need to think. And I feel bad for them. I'd rather you be flexible enough to think deeply about and respond freely to the world around you. I'd rather you focus on your objectives, so I can talk about these ideas—free improvisation, boundaries, abstracted elite expressions with imperceptible forms, or playing elementary forms for commerce—and you can have the facility and flexibility to form a response.

I regularly take my sons to hear jazz. They didn't like it much when they were kids. They'd say, "Oh, man, not this again." In fact, they'd go to sleep most of the time. Once I took them to see Cecil Taylor, a great pianist with an intense sprawling, superelite style. And one of my boys got up on the chair in the back of the Vanguard.

"Wow," he said. He just kept staring. He couldn't believe Taylor. He actually stayed alert for some twenty minutes, transfixed the entire time.

"Are they going to do this for the whole night?" he asked.

"They might," I replied.

"I can't believe that this many people want to hear that."

"Well, that's the great thing about New York."

If it had been New Orleans, a full night of that particular example of structural freedom might be a tough proposition. But you know what? My sons didn't go to sleep on Taylor. Well, eventually they nodded off a bit. But they hung in there much longer than they hung in for most anything else. And I relate this tale not to validate or vindicate their taste. Just to point out the interest, the unexpected interest, that arose that night.

"Hmm, Dad, what is this?"

Freedom, for some.

4

Playing Jazz

July 18, 2003

Dear Anthony,

How are you, man? Glad to hear you got something from my last letter. Don't just read that stuff and lock it away in your head, figure out how to apply it.

Tours go on and on. We just out here, from one city to the next. I just head where they tell me. So excuse the distance between these notes. I try to write when I can.

Man, last night we played a small, intimate club inside a Boston hotel. Can't complain at all; gig just felt good. Small places, man. The people all around you, making all kind of noise and grooving. It just inspires the band. Folks in the audience let the sound wash all over them, especially when our drummer, Herlin, gets sanctified on the tambourine in 5/4.

After the gig, someone brought us a full-course meal—black-eyed peas, corn bread, barbecued ribs, mashed potatoes, even had the nerve to have some corn pudding. People cook for you when you sound good and have good manners. In all seriousness, though, no matter how often something like that happens, and it happens a lot, the love and generosity of spirit that we feel out here is always humbling. And it makes missing your family a bit more tolerable. But boy, if you don't like people, you'll have a lonely time out here.

I wanted to rap with you about playing. Yes, that simply, that essentially—what it takes to play jazz music. Playing covers four essential bases: the expansion of your musical vocabulary, employing charisma in your sound, locating your personal objective, and embracing swing. Let's spend some time chopping all four up.

First, the more vocabulary you know, the more you can play. It's just like talking. A person can know twenty words very well and communicate successfully. But there's gonna be a whole pile of things that he or she never talks about. You need to have vocabulary on all aspects of jazz—melodies, harmonies, rhythms, and personal effects. It's always best to start with what you should know—things from your region, then national things. In other words, if you're from Kansas City, you need to know what the Kansas City blues sounds like. Then you need to know American themes and tunes. And today you need to know more music, especially in the global sense. All over the world, styles of music have specific objectives. Learning those objectives will serve you well, allowing you to incorporate a greater breadth of material into your own vocabulary. Musicians in the Latin tradition always complain that the jazz musicians don't know any of their music. Study and learn whatever music catches your fancy from around the world with people who know it and can play it. The enhancement to your own music will be invaluable. Studying the vocabulary of music is like etymology. If they're interested in romance languages, people will study Latin, from which all those languages descend. In the same manner, most groove music comes from the African 6/8 rhythm—the claves in Cuban music to the shuffle of the Mississippi blues. But if you don't know your own language, your own vocabulary, forget about learning someone else's.

Second, always bring charisma to your sound. People want to *hear* some music. They don't come out to see robots toot horns. They want to be uplifted, amazed, and enlightened. Infuse your sound with charisma. What you do when playing for the public isn't much different from any stage-based performance. Imagine the actor who trots out onstage only to deliver lines in bland fashion with no regard to distinguishing his or her craft. Would that make you enthusiastic? You have to understand and locate your distinct approach to the music, and then infuse your playing with that sentiment. Whatever your approach turns out to be, deliver it with force, power, and conviction. With *fun*, man. This is *playing*.

But while you're up on that bandstand blowing with force and power, keep in mind that playing jazz is like anything else in life: When you start a thing off, you're much more enthusiastic than when you get to the middle. If you're running a race, you shoot out like Jesse Owens reborn. Playing ball? That enthusiasm might make you think you're Joe Montana. Then after a couple of interceptions the thrill is gone. This happens in almost every activity in the world. So when you play, don't get carried away or burned out by the importance of your own effort. Start good. Finish good. Sound good. No more complicated than that. And when I say sound good, I mean sounding good enough to get a job. Because when you sound good, people will hire you; when you sound good, people will be calling.

Of course, sounding good also goes beyond the marketplace; it goes right to the heart of your personal objectives—our third base of playing. Although objectives vary, depending on the individual, there exists a central, common point: What do you want to give to people? Let me lay this on you. Once I asked Sweets Edison, "Why is it that you always sound good, from the first note that you play?"

"There's only one way to play, baby boy," Sweets answered. "There ain't but one way to do it."

Sweets meant that you project your way with the ultimate feeling all the time, whether you're playing in a sad band, a great band, for elementary school students, at someone's birthday party at their house, or 'cause someone fixed a meal for you. When you pull your horn out, you should play as if that's the most important moment in your life. If it's not, make it be.

Remember when you were a kid and you really, really wanted something? It could have been the most trivial thing. Remember the way you begged and pleaded for it? Imagine playing with that passion, that desire, as if this was the most needed thing in your life. When we get older, we learn how to temper our wanting, our desire. Well, tap back into that childhood fervor and freedom of expression. That's what you have to have when you play. That thing you wanted the most and the way you were willing to sacrifice any speck of pride or dignity to obtain it. Remember how you wanted it; remember how you cried when you didn't get it? What about the girl who couldn't stand you? Or who liked you until Amos came around? Play with *that* passion.

Realize that the fundamentals of jazz help you develop your individuality, help you find that passion. Don't say, "I'm not going to really play blues," or "I'm not going to address swing." Don't run from you. Running carries a cost. Have you ever noticed that when you hear a contemporary Latin band play and juxtapose it with a jazz band, the Latin music almost always sounds better? You wonder why that's the case? Just look at the bandstand. You'll see that the Latin musicians appear invested and involved; they believe in the integrity of their groove. Now look at the jazz band: not accepting the swing, trying to find some quasi-funk groove or, even worse, that sad jazz quasi-Latin groove. You can practically hear them muttering to themselves—"Swing is dead; let's try something else." They take detours to avoid sounding bad and run right into what they flee. The fourth and perhaps most important facet of playing jazz, *swing* and swinging.

You may hear about "quintessentially American" things. Well, what makes a thing quintessential is that it reflects the values of the thing it is supposed to be quintessentially about. In the case of an art form, it not only reflects the values, it embodies them, it ennobles them, and it emboldens them. That's why people study art forms with such intensity, because the artist channels the spirit of the nation. In the case of the swing, no one person created it; democracy is a collective experience. And swing is a democratic and *quintessentially* American concept.

Swing is supreme coordination under the duress of time. Swing is democracy made manifest; it makes you constantly adjust. At any given time, what's going to go on musically may not be to your liking. You have to know how to maintain your equilibrium and your balance, even if things are changing rapidly. Swing is designed for you to do that. Why? Each musician has a different concept of time. Sometimes I tell my students, "I want you all to stand up when a minute is over." And some people get up after twenty seconds. Some get up after a minute and a half. That shows the variance between individual concepts of time. As a player you have to, of your own volition, come to a conclusion about how you approach time.

But swing has a hierarchy, like a government. The president of the swing is the drummer. The drummer has the loudest instrument and the cymbal is in the highest register. In African music it's called the bell rhythm. It's always the high rhythm, because you can hear that rhythm. In jazz, the bell rhythm is on the cymbal. You follow the bell rhythm.

But, like a government, swing also has checks and balances, because if the drummer rushes, the bass player might bring the time back. Sometimes the president of the swing is whoever has the best time. When Charlie Parker played, his time was so good that the bell rhythm would follow him. So you have that possibility. This is also a democratic proposition. If you have a weak president, man, you might need a strong legislative branch, or a stronger judiciary—checks and balances.

Swing ties in with the heart of the American experience: You make your way; you invent your way. In jazz, that means you challenge the time, and you determine the degree of difficulty of the rhythms you choose to play. You could play quarter notes, which are difficult to play in time. Or any type of impossible, fun syncopations. Or you could just play strings of eighth notes. You try to maintain your equilibrium with style, and work within the flow. That's what the swing offers.

Listen to a classic record of jazz musicians really playing and swinging, and you'll hear the difference from much of what we play now. Those musicians knew how to play that groove, and the knowledge of that groove has almost been lost. We don't sound as good, and not because there's anything wrong with swing. Rather, the fault lies in the manner in which we play swing grooves. I'll tell you, if the Latin musicians played their music as poorly from a groove standpoint as we play our music, they'd be run out of clubs. But jazz musicians get celebrated for not swinging. I also want you to understand that the act of playing a Latin groove has never been under the type of siege that the act of swinging has been in this country. There have never been battalions of experts to assail the value of clave. We, on the other hand, have the classic American inferiority complex that results in the celebration of all things European or non-American in matters of culture. If we did it, it must be provincial or no good. Folks in Europe had to tell us that jazz was art. And, of course, in our country the dark one always looms on the horizon. He who was shackled in the heart of freedom. The American Negro. His presence brings the battalions proclaiming the death of swing, legions of critics and so-called experts bent on directing people away from the essence of this music, because it was invented by the dark ones and is thus—in their incorrect view—less American.

Why can other forms still celebrate the integrity of their defining cultural music as classic in the face of modern commercialism? I go to Latin countries and funk exists, rock exists; yet, they still play tango. They've got funk in Brazil, they've got all the electronic music we have. Yet, they still play samba. They ain't saying, "Well, let's stop playing all our music to play this." They play the other stuff, and they play the hell out of their own music. Okay, all of the commercialism and stuff comes from us, but still, we play our most sophisticated, defining national grooves like some dreadful, dutiful obligation, when we deal with it at all. And the national dance, swing, has all but disappeared.

Be clear about the point: To play jazz, you have to embrace swing, and the art of swing. It is an objective of a jazz musician to swing. It's a basic, fundamental, and essential component of this music. A group of musicians struggling to elegantly dance improvised melodies in complete rhythmic coordination as each introduces another sense of where the beat should actually be. The ultimate give-and-take is right there, *swing*. I'm telling you this, Antonio; you're a jazz musician. Try to sidestep this notion of not swinging. The unswinging is forced onto the natural inclination of this music, something that disturbs your basic, inner sense of how things should be. Make you walk into a room, and, damn, you walk right out. Then you're going to be in 23/7 or 9/13. You have to start inventing convoluted stuff to create interest because you're not swinging. That stuff you create might be great, but swing in all of its diversity has a specific meaning. It brings the audience into your sound. And the rhythm section has got to, above all else, be swinging, because swing invented the rhythm section. If you're not swinging, then there's no grip. And jazz has to have grip. Not volume-grip.

Let's take things from the general—playing jazz—to the more specific: playing a jazz ballad. Much of the stuff I've laid on you obviously applies here, along with a few other wrinkles, the most important of which is time. Coleman Hawkins said he approached show tunes as if he was making love. You got to have control of time to deal with love, man. The reason Ben Webster, for instance, plays ballads so well has to do with time. It's harder to play in time when the tempo is slow. The beats are bigger and require more investment. You want to float on top of the rhythm section, but you have to direct them even more. With rhythm and sentiment. You have to know, to play slow.

Does that make sense to you? Well, remember when you were a kid and your mama or daddy threw out those big words whose meanings escaped you? Nevertheless, you had enough of an idea of the context those words were used in to allow you to use them, too. Now, you were using the same words, but the meaning wasn't as clear to you. A similar thing occurs when we play jazz. Young cats have heard these things produced by great musicians—tunes, ideas, timbres, and late-night evocations—but don't know any of the underpinnings, the structures, or the philosophies that support those ideas. And because they don't know what lies underneath, when they play, there's an essential component missing.

That underpinning is the fundamental, the root. And training for a thing should revolve around the root. You want to build a house? You go to someone and they say, "Man, this is what you got to do to lay a foundation." After that, the choice to build a labyrinth, a castle, or a shack rests with you, but the fundamentals remain consistent. When you play a ballad, the first fundamental is a romance-love: "My heart is sad and lonely. For you I sigh. For you, dear, only." Maybe that seems hopelessly outdated and corny to you today. I know you haven't seen those ideas running wildly about for a while, if ever. See, when decadence steps up, romance and intellectual pursuit are the first things it pushes down, like when fascists or some other soul-destroying, totalitarian entity comes around. They have to destroy all relationship, all connections to the grandeur of the past so they can come in and tell you who you actually are.

A ballad requires a rhythm section playing a slow dance tempo. Well, you've probably never played for dances, so how do you know how slow people need to dance when they're rubbing bellies, or if they'll even dance to it? For all you know, they might want to go slam dancing. So what do you do? You're a musician. You want to play a ballad. Well, you have to reinvigorate the classic songs. Or you have to write new songs. You have to reinvigorate the romantic sentiment in the culture. You have to do it. If not you, then who? If you don't feel like it's worth revitalizing, don't even consider ballads. If you think the romantic feeling is not worth articulating, then it doesn't make sense to play it, because you won't sound good.

You've got to use all the nuance and shading of your tone to create sounds that make a ballad come alive. And that slow tempo will make you feel stiff. But you can't play stiff—physically, emotionally, technically—while playing a ballad, or anything else for that matter. You have to be open and loose enough to deliver the emotion of something intensely personal to a room of people you don't know.

Keep this in mind when you consider what and how to play: It's your job to listen, learn, and appreciate, not to merely mimic what you've heard by great musicians. All the talk about the tradition, well, that's just something you should know to be a jazz musician. If you and I were doctors, hanging with some other doctors, I wouldn't be sitting up having a discussion with you about whether you should understand the craft. If we were a basketball team . . . well, you just might have to keep going over basic fundamentals, the way cats play these days.

But don't be confused by the talk of fundamentals into thinking that your prime mission is to regurgitate information that you've heard already. That's a typical confusion caused by the dumb stuff too many critics write in the magazines that inform musicians. The fundamentals exist because they exist in every art. When you actually stand up and play, the only thing interesting for me to listen to will be something I haven't heard, something particular to you. It's not interesting for me to hear you play like someone I've heard already, because you're not going to play it as well. It's only interesting to hear you play something that makes me say, "Have mercy! What was that?" because of your unique articulation.

And that's what makes jazz so hard to play. It's difficult to change the status quo. Say I'm used to dealing with you in a certain way all the time. Then one day you come to me and put your hand on my shoulder, something you've never done. And you say, "Man, I need to talk to you about something." Immediately you're going to command my attention in a dramatically different way. I'll have a reaction to you. Why? Because you've never done it before, you've altered the dynamics of our relationship. That's what you try to do with this music. You have to challenge the listener to hear you on your own terms. And the best way to do that is to reveal something y'all both understand to be true but never heard uttered out loud, because nobody had the courage to say it.

Man, I gotta stop. This pen is killing my fingers, plus everybody's fixing sandwiches and arguing about Bush and them. Write back soon, and let me know how this stuff grabs you. I got to cuss somebody out and get me some tuna fish. And Anthony, one last thing: When it comes to playing jazz, don't give up. Ever. I mean that literally. Don't give up on what you're playing. Because when you're up there, you don't know what your playing sounds like. You could think that it doesn't sound good, but it could be some of your best stuff. So don't give up on what you're playing. And always remember what Lester Young said: "If you can't play the blues, you can't play shit."

Sing on.

5

Arrogance of Position

August 2, 2003

Dear Anthony,

Today we set off down the road to Vermont. Warm Daddy
Wes, saxophonist superb, left off making his world-famous
coffee to put on something swinging. The way the music
floats over and through the growling hum of the bus en-
gine can be so strangely relaxing and familiar, like the rum-
ble of purpose mixed with intent.

This morning's listening took me to a question I want
you to ponder: What produces the consistent beauty in the
sounds of people like Charlie Parker, Stan Getz, Miles
Davis, and Sidney Bechet? We listened to Sonny Stitt and

to Joe Henderson. They have totally different styles. Yet, you hear something similar. Even if you go outside of America, you can find that similarity. Jazz stalwarts from all over the world lay claim to that same consistency. Today I want you to walk down that very road. And if you can hold yourself to a higher standard than you hold others, if you can withstand the harsh light of your own scrutiny, if you can triumph over a particular arrogance we all share, perhaps you will meet the consistent beauty at the end of that road.

If you hear Gidon Kremer or Zakir Hussain play, if you hear Maria Callas sing, you realize, of course, that great musicians exist in other traditions. You also hear a consistent richness in their sound. Yet, when you hear Billie Holiday, you hear something else. Not better or worse, simply another type of consistency specific to jazz. Look at trumpet players in the jazz tradition—Louis Armstrong, Roy Eldridge, Dizzy, Miles, Freddie Hubbard, Woody Shaw. We could go into different cultures and produce great jazz trumpeters, like Fats Fernandez, the great Argentinean trumpet player. Even if separated by region, time, or culture, that consistency of beauty still breathes in all their work. What is the thing that ties together all these people who really can play? Well, I'll tell you *where* it is, at any rate. Listen again; it's right in front of you, man, sitting in the emotion of the sound, defining the sheer essence of the music. That's what you need to get in your sound. A glow. So how does one do that?

It starts with recognition. We all spend far too much of our time running away from our central issues. Trying to figure out how to construct a world in which we ignore our insecurities. In jazz, that means that you talk to someone who can really hear harmony well, and, sure enough, they'll prefer to play songs with a lot of change and nothing else; or if you're someone who can play really high, you always want to play high notes. People who rush often play the real fast tunes. People who like swing music put down bebop musicians, and some who love the bebop language will insist theirs is the only language a musician should know.

For instance, talk to the musicians who come out of the Art Blakey school; they will say Max Roach couldn't really swing and that he rushed. You talk to the musicians who like Max Roach; they'll say, "Well, these Blakey guys can play, but they're not playing intelligent enough." Ultimately, everyone wants to construct his or her own truth. Maybe the greater truth is that all these things are true. For your purpose, however, the relative differences of great musicians' styles are less important than what makes them the same. You can learn from Max Roach. You can learn from Art Blakey. The question is: Can you develop your style to address the truth of what you really want to say, and not skirt on the outside with some bogus philosophy or conception? How do you get closer to the thing that you loved enough to leave home?

You're an Oklahoma boy, Anthony, completely removed from the big city. Yet, here you are in New York, trying to play. That's a hell of a sacrifice you've made. But how much more will you sacrifice to get inside yourself, to do what you must in order to get closer? This notion of issue-avoidance goes beyond music. You'll confront it with your friends. You'll confront it with your kids. You see it in America whenever the subject of race comes up. You're going to confront it at one time or another for the measure of your life. How much do I actually love this thing? How much of myself am I going to give up in loving this? Am I going to let go of my insecurities and enter the fray with the full power of my convictions?

As jazz musicians we've stepped into the modern world. And in that modern world our music is defined not by race but by achievement. It's not about the many social conventions that once affected it. Jazz exists on CDs. And millions of people can play them and discuss it. But very few people can *play* it. Not many musicians want to truly look at the music, get inside of it, and keep dealing with it. Eventually we find ourselves influenced by writers, jazz magazines, critics of any old stripe, the apathy of friends, the lack of job opportunities. Musicians are influenced by all kinds of things that have absolutely nothing to do with the music—that's life. Then we're further influenced by a personal desire not to be challenged to the ultimate. To say, "I'm okay because I can play my gig right here. This is good enough for me." Well, don't just accept that. Playing jazz is not a matter of prescriptions, unwavering "Thou shalts" or "Thou shalt nots." It's a matter of understanding what a thing means to you, and being dedicated to playing that even if its meaning casts a cold eye on you yourself.

Let's come back to the question: What is that thing of consistent beauty? And do you want to find it in your own style and sound? To do so, you have to move past the arrogance of your position. I don't mean arrogance with me, or with a teacher, or with your daddy or your mama or whatever you got an issue with. I'm talking about your arrogance with yourself. You know how you might walk past a mirror at the wrong time and see your reflection at an angle that you don't like? An angle that shows you that the certainties you hold about yourself may not be all that rock solid? It's something that basic, man. That one inopportune glimpse into the mirror takes you right past the arrogance of your position.

Jazz music's power comes from its ability to take you deeper into yourself, to a relationship within. A lot of what you see going on today, the quick-fix philosophies and one-step systems, are designed to keep you away from self-discovery. But I want you to go past the arrogance of your position into a love of the sound of the music. And pursue your version of that intangible, consistent beauty you hear in the greats, and pursue a love of yourself.

I was at Carnegie Hall a few years back, listening to some younger cats play with the veteran musician Sonny Rollins. My father and I sat next to legendary bassist Percy Heath, and I remember Heath saying, "I don't know about y'all generation, youngsters." My father had to agree: "Yeah, they don't play like the old ones."

That expectation and production of a certain sound is simply a part of their generation. More of them had it. Many of us don't. It's just one of them things, man. Certainly, youngsters do things that those guys can't and couldn't do. But sound is not one of 'em. Obviously, those guys worked. But what did they work on? What do you work on to get that kind of individuality to come out of your sound? I'm not talking about playing scales. You won't find technical solutions to what we're talking about. I guarantee you that. Look at the way Dizzy Gillespie positioned his horn at his mouth; he may have had the worst embouchure ever. It affected his playing toward the end of his life, but he also had an original sound in abundance. And it's true on the drums, as well. I remember doing a master class with Max Roach, in the eighties. He taught me a piece of his magic, just a touch and a song with the drums (supersoft, man, those cymbals were singing). You had to hear the beauty, just the sound of the instrument itself, the concern. How do you get that? How do you get that smoke in your sound?

It starts with an embrace. As if to say, "I embrace this sound, this style." As soon as you start to embrace that sound, you've made an investment that comes with returns and demands. That's the sign that you're serious. You have to know your old lady's birthday, right? You have to know her favorite food. You have to know the people in her family. But what if you didn't know when your old lady was born? And you don't know how many people are in her family? You have no idea of her favorite food? You don't know about the best teacher she ever had? What if you don't know what floor she works on, the time she goes to work? Well, damn, what do you know? But if you didn't have the basic love or the impulse and desire, if you hadn't made the investment, those facts alone would amount to nothing, except an FBI file.

Much like in jazz. The technical points are simply the facts you know. The love, impulse, and desire lie in the heart—the love heart as well as the courage heart. Say you tell a student to do a long tone, to think about getting the biggest sound with the softest volume and hold each note for one minute. That's not a popular exercise. Students want to play exciting exercises. Producing that long tone just means sitting there with a horn going "hooooo" forever. Who wants to do that? Who wants to listen into a still tone and seek what ye shall find?

Sure, there's technique to a long tone, but that long tone is about you. Today it's more important than ever to stress the spiritual aspects of our art. Without that, jazz lacks meaning. The spiritual component carries meaning, and that's what inspires you to go out and do things. The fact that you really love your old lady makes you want to know all of those things about her. The love is what comes first. Not, "I know these things, therefore I love my lady." I want to play piano. You didn't say, "I want to play the C-major scale. I would love to play chord substitutions. I want to study the style of Thelonious Monk." You might say, "I love Monk's sound." But your first impulse is spiritual. "I want to create that feeling with my sound."

A pristine technique is a sign of morality. If you don't want technique, you can't really be serious. You'd be like the guy who comes to a game out of shape. The other team will just run you to death and exploit you as the weak link. You thought you were rebelling against the team regimen, but now you see that your laziness was really self-crippling stupidity. Don't start professing a love for the game. The love is what would have made you get your ass in shape.

And love is the spiritual essence of what we do. Technique is the manifestation of the preparation and investment as a result of the love. Take Bach: Walk 250 miles to hear a great organist perform. No problem. I love it so much my feet don't hurt. Or Beethoven: goes deaf, can't hear anything. He gives up writing music for long periods of time, questions whether it's worth dealing with at all, experiences epic frustration. Then, deep into one painful silent night, he gets up, pulls out a piece of paper, and says, "Let's see." But now it's even deeper, more resolute. A love that's been supremely tested.

Think about what great musicians go through to play their music. Think about what Duke Ellington went through: segregation, prejudice, ignorance, the amount of his own money that he had to spend to keep the band together. Man, there's always a large helping of pain underneath anything great. Look at the casualties of this music. Lester Young, the great tenor saxophonist, drank himself to death. He was so stricken by the injustices he experienced in the military during the forties that it affected him for the rest of his life. Coleman Hawkins, practically the father of the tenor sax. He too drank heavily and died of liver disease. The way Bird died. Monk, who just became a recluse, lost his mind. Columbia Records asking him to record Beatles tunes. Look at all the guys. We could go on and on, produce a roll call of people. In the long run, the way these men died was no way to go out, man. And it sho's not what they wanted. Gerry Mulligan once said to me, "Damn, this music, it pulls a lot out of you." Those words were so true, so painfully true.

These men did not die because they couldn't face life and had to turn to one vice or another, but because they had to deal with something so intense that it burned them up. They couldn't handle the intensity of their work and the intensity of the irrational opposition to the fact of greatness coming from them. John Lewis once asked me, "How do you handle the pressure?" I laughed it off, and he admonished me, saying, "Don't make light of it, because it will wear you down and destroy you. Charlie Parker and those guys were all young men with high-minded aspirations."

There's something in what all those musicians said and felt about the opposition to them and their music. And it's real, this thing that stands against what this music offers. From Scott Joplin's time, through Bird, Duke Ellington, and up to the current day, we've been fighting forces, whether individual or institutional, that are hostile to the truth of jazz, an inherent truth about the Negro in America and the reality of that experience—the blood-soaked pain at the root of our country, the remarkable resilience, the democratic compact that encompasses all of America, the production of genius under duress. The great walking encyclopedia of Americana Phil Schaap said that the first national pastime to integrate was jazz, not baseball.

If jazz speaks the truth of those things, what about America and the Negro? What should America do? What can it do? It's easier to say that the civil rights movement answered those questions. Or observe that since the Negro doesn't support any art, what difference does he make? For many, it's easy to run from the music's truths, or attack its core by redefining jazz out of existence. One American newspaper even went so far as to proclaim: "The great innovations in jazz now all come from Europe." Boy, you talk about trying to escape. When you change the paradigm of jazz, when you kill it, the nation alleviates another portion of its guilt about how it has treated the Negro.

But that only takes another step away from solving the great American problem. How do we embrace ourselves? How do we come together with the best part of our past? That's what the *Jewish Daily Forward* asked in 1919 when they heralded James Reese Europe's parade up Fifth Avenue in acknowledgment of the sizable Afro-American contribution in World War I. That's really what Benny Goodman asked in his 1938 Carnegie Hall concert when he performed with members of the Basie and Ellington bands. That's what Duke thought about when he wrote "New World A-Comin'." That's what Pops had in mind when he hired Jack Teagarden to play trombone with the All Stars when most of America was segregated. That's what Coltrane was getting at with *A Love Supreme*. Charles Mingus with *Fables of Faubus*. Max Roach with the *Freedom Now Suite*. Sonny Rollins with *Freedom Suite* and Dave Brubeck with *The Real Ambassadors*.

Antonious, you have to understand this truth about jazz, and realize why it has that kind of opposition. And why musicians have fought so hard to counter that opposition. When you can understand and see, then you will be much closer to this music. But as long as you can't see, if you don't understand that the opposition's there, if you aren't interested in what all of these people were talking about, if it's not real to you, you will never find that thing. You have to be moved to the point of feeling you have absolutely no choice but to question all the bullshit and pursue the truest truth you find. To step past the arrogance and into the embrace of your sound. Then, inevitably, that thing will come up in your sound. Then you will find your place in the center of the music's soul and touch a piece of that consistent beauty. And no one else can do anything about it, except be angry. Or happy.

In the words of that great Irishman, W. B. Yeats: "Daybreak and a candle end."

It's 6:00 in the morning, man . . .

6

Who Keeps the Gate?

August 14, 2003

Dear Anthony,

How goes it? Man, your last letter caught me by surprise. You sounded so genuinely angry I had to read it twice. And all because of that article you sent along? Hey, I read it. Didn't stir me much, but I guess I've become used to it. Don't let criticism you read or hear of me shake you none. It doesn't bother me. Why should it bother you? In fact, the criticism makes me feel good because it's actually a sign of respect. Not respect for my music—frankly, I don't think most of these fellas have really heard my playing—but a sign of respect for who I am in the culture. Over the years the criticism has seldom attacked my actual music, just someone's notion of what I represent. Anyway, what if you never got attacked, only celebrated? Man, that would be boring. Hey, get used to a good drubbing, too, for your own part, if you want to pick up this charge of standing against the tide. Everyone has to face some sort of criticism. The question is, what will yours be?

When critics get on me, you'll hear them toss the word "gatekeeper" about, as though I stand barring entrance to the hallowed pantheon of jazz. In truth, the criticism has nothing to do with that, either. Look, with intelligent people, certain agendas have to be couched, camouflaged. And the thing the agenda gets couched in is seldom the issue. Folks rile about affirmative action. Affirmative action is not the issue. The issues stem from slavery. The issues are competition for jobs, education, compensation, and a tradition of being denied. But the term "affirmative action" assumes a life of its own. Then it means quotas. But it doesn't mean quotas. It means a proactive relationship with people who have been denied access. Few, however, will discuss the issue in those terms. They'd rather discuss quotas and the Bakke decision. Anthony, words take on lives of their own and end up having little to do with what they actually represent. Bottom line, the same people without jobs. And don't think that a black issue is not everyone's issue.

When jazz critics attack me and call me a gatekeeper, I'm always tempted to say, "Of what?" They say I'm the establishment. How can one man or one small organization be *the* establishment, with thousands of jobs, magazines, critical discourse, history, and tradition? All of that is jazz. Have they all given up being the establishment to let me run things? Hmmm. Maybe a certain type of bourgeois critic naturally rebels against what he perceives as middle-class or upper-middle-class structures. He's still just rebelling against himself. And what better to rebel against than the supposed establishment led by a Negro? That's a twofer, like hiring a black woman.

It's also a head fake. The establishment is who's mad. In truth, the entire notion belongs in the strange dialogue of race, jazz, and America; it belongs in the answer to who really keeps the gate. Do musicians? Or do people and institutions who've made it their business over the decades to tell cats what they should play and say. Here's a good example of a verbal head fake: Musicians in New Orleans invent a style of music that celebrates freedom. They call it "ragtime" or "jazz." Somehow it gets renamed "dixieland." Now, dixie is the opposite of freedom to a Southern black musician. But there it is, on the name of their music (and nobody asked them). If a man in an interview were to say, "I don't play 'dixieland' and don't like dixie," there he goes trying to be the establishment or just being difficult. You know how he is (wink wink).

Let's talk about how and why, outside a dedicated core of musicians and artists, jazz is devolving. I've seen the phenomenon running rampant at so many of the festivals at which we've played. And it has much to do with our contemporary definitions about jazz, and who makes them. Every art form has a meaning, and a great deal of time gets spent contemplating that meaning, figuring out how to delve deeper. We could be talking about forms from samba to flamenco, hundreds of forms of music, each with its advocates, formal education, and students. Some forms evolve and cross-pollinate with other forms. Schools of thought spring up. People spend their time writing books and analyzing. In the end, a community of artists and scholars orbit a defined meaning and concentrate on levels of taste.

But if all of these art forms have some meaning discernible enough for them to be taught, why not jazz? Man, as Geoff Ward says, "jazz seems like the only word in the English language with no meaning," or a meaning so broad it includes everything. I don't know of another music form with a definition so broad, so fluid, that any essential meaning itself vanishes, or of one with so many supposed advocates happy with that state of affairs. So I pound a funk beat all night, but I've got a horn section; I'm playing jazz. I play electronic rock, but with a cat on the sax; I'm playing jazz. Some rappers roll out a few instruments, toss a horn solo on top; they're playing jazz. Well, what is jazz, then?

Now, the real jazz, with people playing and swinging over form and blues, certain so-called experts say that's old and dead. They say that jazz today must achieve a state of perpetual innovation, with no achievement meriting contemplation or possessing lasting value. A fast-food art form. Perhaps that statement makes it seem like I'm against valuing innovation. Actually, I encourage knowing what something means so you'll know whether you're innovating to begin with. If you don't understand the meaning of a thing, how can you possibly innovate in it? And if it actually doesn't mean anything, why waste your time innovating in it?

Jazz has been watered down. And the curious thing with the process, all these alternative definitions of the music never build it up, they always amount to less—less blues feeling, less swing, less improvisation in the context of harmonic forms that require the use of vernacular melodies. You're fed the illusion of more freedom, and you get less jazz. Yet, enhanced freedom was supposed to bring you more jazz. If you have more freedom, why is there less jazz? Where did the jazz go? Where does it rest?

Well, the experts say, the jazz was all the older cats. They could play jazz. But they're gone. Now we supposedly have more freedom. So what should we teach younger people? Do we want them to play the jazz that older cats played because the experts and critics say those are the only people who played it? But *that* jazz doesn't mean anything anymore, according to the same cognoscenti, since it embodied those good ole hallmarks of swing and the blues and a soulful tone now deemed archaic. Or do we want young people to have more so-called freedom? So, young cats, your "more freedom" equals less jazz, but that's okay, because jazz is meaningless, anyway. How do you teach someone with that philosophy? Well, here's the punch line: Don't teach it. And if it doesn't propagate, then jazz has got to be dead, right? But if that's the case, why is everything jazz? How can it be dead and yet be in everything, like salt?

The point is: Critical institutions have codified a definition of jazz that works like assisted suicide, since jazz exists only in the form of deceased masters or in styles that have almost no jazz in them. There's no more jazz—hallelujah! You are free to play other cultures' music badly and call it jazz, to play any form of backbeat music and call it cutting-edge jazz, any style imitating European avant-garde music and call it new jazz. But don't come in here swinging or with some blues. That alone among the jazz establishment is what must be stopped, because it's been done before by great jazz musicians before you. Wow! Talk about dixieland. Bring me a hot toddy! Let's dilute the music further to help it die. I contend that that was the objective all along. Don't teach it, because it brings you back to that great truth, and that great truth will battle that great lie. And the great lie is that there are people who by birth are objectively inferior to other people and who deserve to be mistreated, and that's a belief that has nothing to do with race, man. It's played out between races in this age, but at another time it might be between genders or tribes. But this music, jazz music, comes to say "God chooses." No group or hairstyle decides who delivers the message.

How do these two forces that we've talked about reconcile? An ever growing, ever burgeoning critical mass of young, hungry-to-play musicians existing right alongside the dilution. I know it seems like a conflicting reality, but it's always been the reality. When Duke Ellington wrote his music, someone said he was writing jungle music. Many condescended to Louis Armstrong's playing. But there were also people saying, "Check out Armstrong."

Unfortunately, this era has fewer advocates. Thus, more stress lies on the people who want to be serious. Our culture has experienced a decline of intellectual rigor along with an unchecked decadence. When there's a greater degree of decadence, a higher level of heroism is required to combat it, because there's much less reward. And if you're serious, you run the risk of falling apart and crumbling because of the stress. It can kill you over a sustained period of time. When you're young, you hold the illusion that what you do will make a tangible difference in what you see. But while you're doing whatever you're doing, your antagonists are enacting their agenda as well. They don't stop what they're doing just because you're pursuing your game plan. That's the beauty of it. The criticism helps test your seriousness, and if you are truly serious, they don't stop. When they stop, you've either become the icon of icons or have been put out to pasture like Uncle Remus, who looks at the girls but "him don't touch."

That dixieland fact may seem greatly ironic to you, Anthony, when you take America's democratic proposition into the equation. Where does all this anti-jazz pressure stem from, when so many people, especially white people, have practically adopted jazz as America's classical music? Yet, there's an undercurrent, an adversarial undercurrent that has existed at least since Jelly Roll claimed he was ripped off by his publishers all the way to today's phenomenon of writing the Negro out of the equation or freezing him in classic amber. But that's the reality of American life, the music of our history. It plays in cycles—Civil War, then Reconstruction; the civil rights movement, then the Republican Reclamation.

In our history, black and white come toward one another, and then we move apart. But each time, we come closer the next time that same point on the circle rolls around. But even in our current jazz time, things don't fall into a neat racial equation. I tend to talk about "The Negro" because it's a particular archetype of both jazz's and America's race narrative, something identifiable, and some white folks like black folks and some don't and vice versa. But, look man, truth be told, very few black people have an interest in jazz, or in any art.

And it isn't just jazz. Look what happened to the church music. You listen to any contemporary gospel of late? They rockin' and booty-shakin' like it's Saturday night. Who else's church service is a national joke in everything from rock videos to basketball-shoe commercials. Next thing, you'll see them in church getting naked. The sanctity of that experience has been slowly watered down. You know, we take the oil out of the ground, and we think there's a lot of it to go around. But it will run out. It's not infinite. What have we got left? A hundred years? When the last of those years rolls around, that will be it. Let's solve problems now. Especially with our culture. I don't think decline is inevitable. I never have. We can and will change things. You young musicians have to have something to do. And we'll talk about that more.

But not tonight. I'm heading to bed. You should go practice, then think about saving the world.

I'm out.

7

Music and Morals

August 31, 2003

Dear Anthony,

These letters are always about music and the type of philosophical wrestling that you wouldn't wish on your enemy. But even though we talk about these things most of the time, I hope you're doing all right, just personally, I mean.

But look, man, you can't hit me with all those big questions when I'm trying to relax the brain at day's end. You had a good one at the close of your last letter. You must be trying to take me out into the ocean. No one's quite asked me whether or not I thought all abstraction was corruption. You must have been musing over all those notions about freedom, structure, and abstraction we talked about a few weeks back. Well, I have no problem with abstractions. In fact, I'm telling you to *play* the most abstract music you can find. My father always told me this coming up: "If you ain't been there, you're guessing." Every experience helps your overall development. But I'll drop a big question for you to ponder now, one that goes to the heart of our Western artistic concept: Is abstraction necessarily more advanced than the thing that it's abstracting, and is there a possibility of a corrupting over-refinement in the abstraction? In other words: Is *Finnegans Wake* eminently more sophisticated than *Macbeth*? Is Arnold Schoenberg's music more advanced than Beethoven's Fifth Symphony, and more satisfying? Is the abstract statement more modern? And is corruption only tied to intent? Let's talk about abstraction, corruption, and the very notion of morality in music.

Ask me about corruption and context will govern my answer, because much depends on what norms have conditioned us to feel. For instance, when Lester Young played in a style different from Coleman Hawkins's, a lot of people thought that was corruption. When Monk played blues dissonances on the piano, again, many people regarded that as corruption. When Duke Ellington began writing more sophisticated music, longer forms, people viewed that as a sign of corruption, because a jazz band was supposed to play dance tunes. Anything that wasn't a dance tune was pretentious. Check history and it'll show you numerous instances of this sort, where corruption appears as the bastard child of the insightful exposing weaknesses in the status quo. But I've always thought real corruption spirals from intent.

That's why the greatest musicians, regardless of the idiom, produced their best work when they were doing the very best they could. It's why Igor Stravinsky could never have been a great popular songwriter. Sometimes it's easy for a jazz musician to think he can just go into pop music. "Here's this Paul McCartney song," you think. "It's not as sophisticated as what I'm used to dealing with, so I can just jump in here and do this." Well, that's a grave error. In order to be great at a thing, you have to be doing the best you can do. Your intent can't come from a place of condescension. That's why so much of jazz-pop music is almost always sad.

One of the more common examples of corruption by intent is pandering to the marketplace: "I don't believe in this, but I want to make me some money, so let me do this. Let me go with the fad." A lot of musicians did that in the seventies. We heard them. And now that music is not a major part of their legacy. Miles Davis's classic is *Kind of Blue,* not *On the Corner* or even *Bitches Brew.* That's not a matter of philosophy. That's just what has happened over the years.

But you can also pander to the intellectuals; you can pander to the academy: "I don't want to pander to the marketplace, but I do want to get good reviews." Or maybe you say, "I want to be a part of this clique, so I'll adjust my playing in this manner."

Pandering to the marketplace or the academy is commonplace because it leads to clear rewards. But corruption certainly creeps in when you pander to your own deficiencies: You can't play fast, so no one should play fast. You can't play slow, so ballads are not worth playing. You can't play on changes, so changes are outmoded. You can't play a freer, fluid form of expression, so no one else should. I suppose the central issue comes down to the fact that we don't have a conception of morality in music. What would that be? Morality lives on a slippery slope anyway. But in an era that regards morality as a relativistic and repressive notion, where freedom is held up as the coin of the realm, morality is in trouble. In most instances morality butts heads with freedom. If there's a morality, who's going to enforce it? If there's an enforceable morality, how can you be free?

Anyway, in our era, it's probably impossible to sell out to the marketplace, because you have to have something to sell out. And how can a person from an era devoid of integrity in music sell it out? In fact, you were born to sell out. How many times have you heard the phrase, "Well, he did what he had to do"? That's the mantra of our times: Hey, baby, just doin' what you got to do. And if you make some money doing it—

okay, even better. As a matter of fact, the value of your work is assessed in economic terms. "How much did it sell?"

I've related your challenge before: to be in your time and to fulfill the needs of your listeners with a well-developed, clear vision of how wonderful this music can be, or is. I don't know how you'll fulfill those needs. You will. My role is to point out your task and opportunity. Playing scales or knowing when a time signature changes, that's something you should just know how to do. (I know: You think I sound like a broken record with this technical thing.) You have to answer the deeper, larger, more philosophical issues.

Here's a story about John Coltrane and Sonny Rollins when they were young men, just before the blooming of their full talents. One would say to the other, "Man, we want to play some music so powerful that it'll actually change the world for the better." Can you imagine two people with that type of talent, and with that type of ambition—an ambition to make music so powerful that it will change things so thoroughly, so completely? That's the crux of the difference between their playing and the playing of other people. Coltrane and Rollins believed and wanted to create jazz of such power, their desire thrust them in the direction of mastery. That's the impulse and the goal: to be creative on that level. Not, "I want to make sure that I can get me an SUV."

As we raise more ideas and your growth continues, I'd

love to see this deeper level of engagement with the times in which you live, with the culture, with the city, with the country, with the world. That engagement, that conversation, sets the stage for your playing because when you begin to play, you gotta set talk on the shelf. What would you say while you're playing? This is the time, man. You're learning. You're going to school. Talk happens here. Much like Rollins and Coltrane talking about what they intended. But once they started the doing, the time for talk had passed. Talk has great value. It helps you settle your philosophy and perceive the reality about you. But playing is playing. And what you play will be defined by your intent.

When you play, make sure you're honest enough to confront your own deficiencies. That's why practicing is a sign of morality in a musician. It means that you're willing to subject yourself to self-scrutiny of the highest order. And, with your music, contemplate the corruption in your time and your relationship to it. Don't allow the status quo to rob you of your point of view. Profound thought and daring action will determine the degree of heroism in your sound, like the hugeness of spirit in Martin Luther King's voice, or the timbre of Louis Armstrong's horn. Heroism is the ability to confront hardship with grace.

How do you confront the corruption of your time? First, you have to identify it and be accurate about it. Corruption's not holding up a sign saying, "I'm corrupt." Corruption's usually disguised, trying to pass itself off as liberation: "Come, this will free you." Identifying corruption when you grow up in a time where it's the norm, where it masquerades as the standard, will be difficult for you. I realize it appears that way to you. But the task may be simpler than you think. How can you tell when something is really corrupt? It brooks no criticism. Like Marcus Roberts used to say, "When you're raised on food, you don't mind dessert. When you're raised on dessert, you don't want to hear about no food."

Today corruption sits most often in the heart of our new American way, where the absurd reigns, an absurdity morphed beyond the point of any recognition, to the point that some conflate it with integrity. In reality, the word "integrity" can be applied to very little that we send out into the world. We simply cling to commercial integrity: the right to put whatever we want into the marketplace, and charge as much as possible for as little as possible. Look at most films: Kill each other left and right, get naked for no reason, and forget about plot while we're at it. Music? Heavy doses of bullshit made by nonmusicians. You know, I've got a tale for you. Here's what happens when you reach the point of perfect absurdity.

I go into an elementary school. The teachers say, "Oh, the school has put together a little thing for you this morning." A little boy, TeShawn, comes out rappin' and starts grabbing his johnson. I ask the teacher, "Is he grabbing his johnson?" She replies, "That's what they do nowadays." I go into a middle school, and the band director comes up and says, "My band, we worked on a song." You know the song they worked on? "Give It to Me." You worked on that? Give *what* to me? Perfectly absurd. Someone throws out the excuse, "That's what the kids want to play." That's what they want to play? Well, who's teaching them? This is the inevitable result when your culture does not hold itself to a standard of integrity. And how do young people, as products of the culture, recognize this fact and act against it? How do you sift integrity from corruption and absurdity if no one takes the responsibility to tell you, to show you?

The degree of conformity to the absurd must be the thing that shocks me most from my travels about the country. I talk to thousands of different people who all spout the same conformity, relevant to their particular program. What's happened in America? Did a machine stamp folks on the forehead right off the conveyor belt? Niches don't make a difference, either. It just changes the shading on the conformity. The jazz musicians all have their jazz thing they hold to. The hip-hop people clutch their hip-hop thing. African Americans, white folk, liberal, conservative—everyone holds a script, like traveling herds of B actors auditioning for a fixed set of roles. And if you don't belong to one of those groups you're going to be put in one.

What happens when whatever integrity you hold fast to runs up against the lack of integrity in the culture in which you have to define yourself? Unless you're a prophet, what gives you the right to say, "That lacks integrity"? Can you hold absolutist standards, seeing a dearth of integrity when folks do something en masse that you abhor? In today's jazz circles, cats wear jeans to the bandstand. Folks used to wear suits. Why go back to that when you can wear jeans on a gig? Do you think that shows a lack of integrity, coming on a gig with jeans? Yet, it seems absurd to say so, because everyone comes to a gig with jeans on and it won't affect how you sound.

I'll raise the stakes some. When I was in high school, I had a friend who worked at a restaurant. He might have been sixteen or thereabouts. He did busboy duty. Most of the other guys who worked alongside him in that restaurant were grown men, cats with families. The man in charge of the waiters and the busboys liked to mess with them, calling them "Niggers" or "Boy" and other Southern terms of endearment. At an unencumbered sixteen, my friend could have chosen to leave, could have trusted that he would get another job. As a matter of fact, he did end up getting fired because he wouldn't take the bullshit. But one of the older fellas who worked there couldn't face that risk. Remember, this was New Orleans in the seventies— a city undernourished with jobs. The guy's got four, five children. He doesn't like the abuse, but it's not as simple for him as trusting fate. So he suffers his humiliation, swabs the knife cuts to his personal integrity. But is he going to let his family starve just because he's being humiliated?

Integrity in the decisions you make won't always be as simple as whether you trust yourself, whether you trust your perception of what's going on. Decisions on integrity become questions of survival, even in situations less dire than feeding your family. Survival can stretch beyond the job, delving deep into the personal, the way we view ourselves, the validation or lack thereof that others show us. Do you want to be ostracized for your integrity? Are you gonna be the preacher of your truth, have everyone around you grumbling, "Man, here he comes again with that shit." Who wants to deal with that constantly? Then integrity can become malleable.

I've had students say that if you really, really trusted and believed in what you thought, you would assume that your viewpoint would eventually become the norm. But I tell them they gotta be bathing in naïveté, because nothing in the history of the world would lead you to that assumption, nothing would make you assume that things naturally become pregnant with a particular person's integrity. And someone, inevitably, will say there must be examples where people have come to respect what folks of integrity did, if only because those people outlasted the opposition.

Maybe. People respected Monk after a while, but where were they when he sat at home for so many years without a gig? Integrity demands hard choices, choices that must be made, choices that you, Anthony, will have to make in your own way. And they don't revolve around right or wrong. They depend on you being equipped to understand your choice, to even understand that you're making one in the first place. When you're in a time with no standard of integrity, you don't know. Things cease being a matter of "I'm going to study this or I'm going to study that." Too often, you simply don't know what you need to do.

I was no less vulnerable than you. For many years I played onstage with a monitor, a choice that kept me from developing my sound. How was I going to know that? Everyone played with a monitor. How do you know something when no one tells you? Or if you just don't listen when an older cat would tell you something. You know what, you drown in your arrogance, thinking, "He don't know. We got a thousand people on a gig, and they play for twenty people."

One day we played a gig in a Greek amphitheater. I was twenty-four at the time, and I'd been playing this way all my life. A guy came up to us, said, "You can't have any electricity in this amphitheater, so you all have to play acoustic." And we started thinking, "Man, we're going to sound like shit playing acoustic." We had never played this kind of music that way. But we had no choice. So we did it. And that was the best gig we ever played because, finally, each of us could hear the other musicians on the bandstand, and not just our own sound pouring back at us through a monitor.

See what the old folks knew?

8

Moving It Forward: The New, New Thing

September 10, 2003

Dear Anthony,

Your last letter actually made me run to the gift shop for
some new stationery and a new pen. Man, you got me
going, because that letter of yours held a question that so
perfectly reflected a great confusion of our time, one that
frustrates so many young jazz musicians as they grow to
maturity. I just had to read it aloud to the guys on the bus:
You wanted to know the importance of creating something new, modern, and forward-looking when you play
jazz, the importance of moving the music forward. That's
frozen tundra you're invading my friend, though it seems
to be the mantra of the modern student. Sit down a sec-

ond; let's talk about what innovation means, and what it does not, and how to avoid this crippling fallacy that befalls young musicians.

We've equated our belief and understanding of art with our view of technology. We think a piece of art is akin to an automobile: This version is better than the Model T. Therefore, we don't need the Model T. Louis Armstrong played through the bebop era up to the rock era. Though he was considered old-fashioned by some, no one replaced him. Coltrane came up with new ways to play harmonies, very interesting things that worked for him. Other people imitated him, and those ideas became part of the so-called "new thing" for the span of time it remained in vogue. But these ideas that Coltrane presented didn't move the art of jazz forward. It wasn't standing still when he arrived. Jazz merely expanded to accommodate his sound. Take those devices out of jazz, and it doesn't go back anywhere. No art does. Perhaps a case can be made for Armstrong moving jazz forward, because he taught everyone in his era to swing. However, the value of his art today is not its relationship to the swing of his times but in the continuing impact of the depth of his music on our souls today. You see, that's why artists speak across epochs. Styles of art change but the technology of the human soul doesn't. How are you going to move past touching the soul?

For all practical purposes, there is no such thing as moving music forward. You can't move it. You suffer from a tremendous illusion if you truly believe you can or hope to do so. And you play into the idea of a generation gap that pits the young against the elders—always a bad idea for both. People don't move music anywhere unless they're on a float. Seek to create a defined place of your own with your music. Bach was considered old-fashioned at the time. But in our time, his world of music is indispensable. Yes, he introduced approaches that didn't exist before him. However, the existence of his music didn't negate or surpass one iota of Palestrina's music. Beethoven's music did not negate the Brandenburg concertos of Bach, or the phenomenal music of Mozart.

Let me go broader. Look at Picasso. Did his style, with his changing forms and completely original ways of looking at fundamentals, surpass the power of artists like Matisse or Goya? I'd say no. Even though his style became the norm for generations of painters. Following him was their choice. Has anyone, even Shakespeare, moved literature forward? Many great writers with different styles have been born, lived, wrote furiously, and died. Did they reveal more of the human character than Homer? Different, yes—but so much more as to make Homer unnecessary or out of mode? I don't think so. In art, there is only one generation, the generation of man. And whether it means a toga, a ruffled collar, a tuxedo, a three-piece, or jeans, it speaks the same language. That's why the arts survive when whole civilizations perish. And remain useful.

As jazz musicians, the great majority of us will not invent a new world of music inhabited by our disciples. Our challenge rests in something we already possess. Our own unique way of playing, as unique as our speaking voice. Now, does that mean you have the potential to be an innovator and create a unique world that becomes the norm for legions? Don't bank on it.

When a student can feel successful only if his or her work rivals the best work of the greatest artist ever, here comes depression, then a philosophy that attacks people who can play, then quitting. Two million people go to law school; you pull out the five greatest lawyers in history and say, "This is the standard of excellence by which you will be judged, pass or fail. If you are not equal to this level, you will not *pass* this course. Now, the first class may be eager to try that. But after the successive generations fail, who in their right mind will want to be a lawyer? So, first, don't think that you will move music anywhere. It's too heavy. And, second, don't feel that your basic level of success as a jazz musician is to be one of the great innovators of all time.

No one can teach you to be an innovator or even discourage you from being one. But someone can teach you to be a fine musician. How is it, given the near impossibility and the obvious absurdity of the goal, that thousands of jazz students all over the world think as you do, Anthony? I've heard that voiced in classes from Savannah to Sydney. "Yeah, we must do something new; must move the music somewhere to be successful." I've heard it for years. And in all those years, how many of those students moved the art form forward? Not one. Their goal killed them. Say I want to get back in shape but I don't articulate the goal that way, to you or myself. I tell you I'm going to be a decathlete and my goal is the 2012 Olympics. And I'm forty-one years old. Man, I probably won't even get in shape, much less make the Olympic team. Now, if I say, "I want to lose thirty pounds and tomorrow I'm going to get up and run a mile and a half, and I will try to go up a half mile every two weeks." Well, I might just lose ten of those thirty pounds in the next month.

When you start out with an impossible thought, you've lost a battle from the outset, unless you're one of the ordained ones, of course. I met Michael Jordan when he was in college. He said, "Man, when I get in the NBA, I'm going to show people what basketball is about!" Me and the other guys in the room just laughed. We thought, "This guy is crazy. He's not even tearing up the NCAA." In this case he knew.

But if you're not the rare ordained individual, you'll fight an unwinnable battle with the crushing weight of your own expectation. You've lost before you've started. The fruitless struggle merely serves to lead you away from your real objective—in our case, learning how to play. Instead of just trying to be good, and learning your instrument, you're set on scaling Everest with no climbing gear. I'd like to hear more musicians saying, "I want to be one of the best trained musicians ever. I want to be able to transpose, I want to improve my reading, I want to be able to play with two hands, I want to play more coherent solos." Now, I'm not advocating unambitious goals, only calling for some reality. Jazz allows for so much creativity for those with fair to good talent. That's one of its greatest strengths. It challenges and accepts people on all levels. But you, Anthony, have a better chance.

You have a better chance of joining the group of great musicians who created their own sound inside of a style—Clifford Brown, Stan Getz, or J. J. Johnson, for instance. I wonder, did anybody tell you to consider yourself a success if you attain your own sound?

Look, Ant, I'm not saying you don't have a chance to be great. But in your training, in your education, in your basic philosophy, if all the members of your field feel good about themselves only if they're on the supreme level, how can anyone feel good about playing? Should all these cats playing Major League Baseball today feel bad about it because they can't play like Babe Ruth? Isn't making the major leagues worth something? You might quit playing from sheer frustration.

What about redirecting your priorities? Instead of "I have to be one of these six great innovators or I'm not a success," you could say, "Hey, these are six great people. And I strive for that same level of power; at worst I would like to develop my own distinct sound." Thinking of Ornette Coleman might be instructive here. Coleman, even in the pantheon of innovation, rings unique. You may imagine him being consumed with matching the legacy and likes of the Louis Armstrongs of the world. You may imagine him competitive in the modern sense. You imagine him taking aim at a summit occupied by other names in the effort to achieve his own glory, his own recognition. But you have to think past our era, where self-promotion becomes the achievement. One of the hardest things to do is think across eras, to another time when people aspired to different things.

Coleman didn't set out to be as great as Armstrong, or anyone else. He once told me, "Music is not a race, it's an idea." Coleman tried to play in a way that would gain him respect from the people he considered peers. That remained his concern; the same concern held by a Paul Desmond or a Cannonball Adderley. Now, as things turned out, many musicians didn't respect what Coleman played. So he had to fight for his identity. And he maintained his identity and his way of playing regardless of what musicians said about him.

When Ornette's group took the bandstand in New York, they'd look up and, wow, there's Wilbur Ware, there's so-and-so. Peer respect meant something to them. Maybe they didn't mouth that concern openly. But you hear it in their music. You see it in their practice philosophy, and in all the things they did to work their concepts up. They were serious about presenting that music for New York. They didn't stay in Texas. They didn't stay in Los Angeles, or whatever other hometowns they had. They wanted to be in New York because the people who could play were in New York. You became a jazz musician in the Apple.

For all of Ornette Coleman's brilliance, and he is a brilliant musician of the highest order, he became one of the first wave of musicians to mainly play his own music, in his own context. Although he gave us an interesting and new way to approach playing melodies and addressing form, that was the beginning of the demise of a standard. And this is how things change. Did he move the music forward? I don't think so. That's why I like to think about Duke Ellington's concept of total jazz. Ornette's way of playing just becomes another part of the complete package. Not *the* new way to go.

I don't relate all of this to say that you can or will be an innovator like Coleman, or that you won't. You alone know what you can be and what you are capable of. But I do know that if your expectation for yourself far outweighs your talent, as the time passes and it becomes more and more apparent to you that you won't reach your goals, you'll get discouraged and quit. Now, quitting doesn't mean that you'll give your horn up. Quitting means that I might see you with a strange hairstyle. Or I might see you with some new jazz clique somewhere.

Never quit. Because whether or not you reach your goal as a musician, you can always participate significantly in this music. Always act in accordance with what you know. Don't adjust your philosophy to your limitations or failures. Never quit. Focus on becoming a good musician. I want you to want that. Invest in your discipline, your practice, and your personal growth. Develop your soul by participating in the lives of other people in a positive way, through giving. You know, some people think the Boy Scouts are corny, but they have a community-service component. They might be focused on going for merit badges or winning jamborees, but a Scout has to go do something for the community as well. That's an important concept, because it means that activities must also have an objective of the soul. And that's what can heal our whole nation. We need *soul* objectives on a high level, a level higher than the pursuit of money and one-upmanship over another person.

As Art Blakey said, "You never see an armored car following a hearse." Be serious about these tasks and you'll earn the respect or jealousy of your peers. And if genius plans to meet you down the road, you won't miss the introduction, man.

In the Sweet By and By.

9

Lone Man on the Prairie

September 22, 2003

Dear Anthony,

You must think me an ornery so-and-so. Earlier tonight I sat quietly in the front lounge of the bus. Most of the guys had long passed into sleep. I swear cats snore differently when their bodies travel in the direction of home. Thought I would get writing done on some music we need to play next month. Instead, I found myself thinking of the road over the last several weeks, of all the missives going back and forth between us. I've given you strong opinion after strong opinion, but I wonder if I've done a good enough job of telling you why. I don't know, man. Maybe I'm tired. Maybe it's the hour, the moment when you feel comfortable enough to reflect upon the things *you* might even be running from. That's why it's important to talk these over, and sometimes over again, because you're on this road with me, Anthony. And that particular highway, the one bordered by hope and belief? That one gets lonely.

You ever wonder what happened to us? Me. You. Our respective generations. Black people. White people. America. Ever wonder what would have happened had we developed the stronger parts of our foundation? What if we as Americans had a mythology that celebrated the best of our country instead of the worst? If our national story celebrated people coming together rather than exploiting the cracks in the collective soul? It may have started with the slavery of the Negro. But at some point, the mind-set becomes slavery for us all; it holds hostage our society at large. As they say about swinging that 'ting, because him cut both ways.

I'll tell you something else. Folks, by and large, don't say, "Well, I ate this pie, so let me go ahead and eat five hundred pies. I'm just gonna wallow in fat." Oh, no! You're going to get up the next day and try to exercise; but you might be locked in that pattern of eating for years before you change it. Indeed, you might never come to grips with it. But you hold the desire to improve. And that desire is exploited everywhere in the American marketplace, man. Get this. Buy that. Improve yourself. Yet somehow this philosophy escapes us in matters of culture.

We seem locked in our cultural basement, where we teach our young the most unthinkably dumb shit. For the girls, the cutting edge is showing as much of your naked behind as possible. For the boys, a celebration of pimping: Everyone in the world pimps, so you got to get yours.

The arts allow you to make thoughts into actual material; they allow you to enable bullshit, or disable it. At times you're in the position where you go along with what everyone's doing, and it's a groove for all. Other times you might have to be the whistle-blower, a veritable pain in the behind. But those carrying on with the groove are going to seem to have a much better time than you because there are so many more of them.

Perhaps I'm a cultural pain in the ass. It isn't a position that I consciously chose. You just see things a certain way and refuse to cower to commonly held points of view. I remember thinking the stuff we played back in the seventies was some bullshit. I wrote that in my senior yearbook. I just knew. I had fun doing it, too. I wasn't on the bandstand mad. But even then I could see what that degradation did to people, the ramifications of the gradual dissolution of standards. I'd played that stuff since I was thirteen; I knew. But it still felt great.

Now I'm forty-one, and when I talk to teenage brothers, I so clearly see the effect on them from what we did in that time. An unraveling has to begin somewhere, and today anyone can see the shredded drawers on the ground and the proverbial johnson exposed. And what you see is not blinding by any stretch of the imagination. Things could have turned a whole other way. Maybe you think I'm overly wistful and full of sentiment, but I really believe that. Things could have turned out another way. And I don't mean turned to some restricted, shackled, puritan place. I don't mean a place where you give up the things you desire, the freedoms you associate with modernity. Damn, you could have more. But they didn't have to be exploited or reduced to base caricatures. Things didn't have to go the way of thuggery, hate, violence, and vulgarity.

But don't get me wrong, I have got hope because of younger people like you. I just don't know why you're not the kid that folks talk to, see, or even imagine when they form an assessment of where young America is heading. Man, I know you got guidance; you got someone you been talking to since you were born. With my daddy, I was lucky: He always told me what bullshit was. And you know what it is, too—somebody told you. You ain't waiting around for me to tell you. I don't care what the conventional wisdom says. I've met many like you, of all stripes. So where do all these boys with daddies—or some tangible leadership—figure into the equation when people harp on about black pathology this and that? All that attention to pathology creates more of it. I guess that's the point. The black artist is the only one whose quality is assessed in terms of pathology. Everyone else's quality gets assessed in terms of the power of their ideas. With us, it's, "Did you live?" Shit, everybody on Earth is living. And the question of living for a brother becomes, "Is your daddy with your mama? Did you get high? Did you have to shoot someone?" Too many Americans of all persuasions have become comfortable with the notion of brothers rolling in the mud of some pathology. But with a brother who ain't coming from that? Who don't want to mess nobody up? Who's not pimping? Now that brother has to prove to people that he's real?

We got a bunch of young cats riding this bus with us right now. One of them, Kwame, reads and studies all the time. I remember his mom taking him to gigs constantly; taking him to lessons all hours of the day and night. So Kwame ain't a brother? All day we're going to hear about someone who got shot or who robbed someone. That's black life? You got little choice about hearing it, with all the media organs living to exploit that crap over the airwaves. But can't people hear the sound of the Kwames out here? Doesn't his life count as black life? He's playing a gig tonight. What he plays on the piano ain't real? He doesn't count?

I talk to young brothers. I play ball with these kids. I see them at schools. Man, I'm around young brothers all the time. I've never lost the connection. I tell them, Look man, we don't need all them hard, ugly-faced looks. I'm not going to try to prove anything to you. You need to prove it to me because I know more about this than you. And the fact that you feel life has messed you over, so what, man? That's unfortunate. But that don't give you license to act all messed up to anyone else. Things happened to me, too, but it has *nothing to do with you.* So the obsession with realness and ghetto authenticity that has a vise grip on black popular culture—that's like volunteer slavery, trying to prove you really did come from the plantation. Brothers need to be out here trying to compete for jobs and education. And whatever our cultural program is, maybe we should be trying to define that in the highest terms instead of the lowest, instead of being a caricature of a black person, try to be a real person. Don't be a toilet for society or fodder for the growing prison business.

Look man, I'm just who I am. I talk to anybody. I don't talk to brothers in another language. Or fall into that old fake cussing and acting an ass. By now you know my speech is a tad colorful; but when I get in that environment, I become more correct, less vulgar. Because I'm trying to say this is not what we're about. I say it anywhere, man. There's nowhere I won't go. Some people are afraid of black people because they only encounter them in the media. But how could *I* be? I love America. We all need guidance and leadership in the cities and the suburbs. They're thirsting for it in these groups I talk to around the country—young brothers just dying. They want a man to look at them with some love in his eyes and say, "This is what you need to be doing and let me help." And it don't have to be a black man. Many times it's not, too.

I do all the schools and programs I can, even if it feels like a drop in the bucket. *You* have to find the significance. Man, it's like fighting when you know you're going to get your butt whipped. You'll feel quite different after you fought and took that ass-whippin' than if you would have lain down. You can get up and say, "Well, that's all right, I was in there." Every drop helps. Every drop has meaning. Every gesture has meaning, despite the fact that the great "how things really are" tries to make you feel as though you're spitting into the wind.

Stanley Crouch and I had a saying in the early eighties: Lone man on the prairie with a shotgun. He's just some keen-sighted motherfucker on the prairie with a shotgun defending the indefensible. He knows he can't stop it; but there he is sitting tall in the saddle against the Big Sky. People come out to laugh at him sitting there in the rain.

"What you doing, mister?"

"I'm defending this."

"Defending what?"

"All of this. Everything you see."

Yup, that's him: the lone man on the prairie with a shotgun in his hand—sworn enemy of bullshit.

You see, the lone man is not trying to blame anyone. He's not looking for the guilty. He's just defending territory, a lot of it.

Anyway, so far as this cultural slime we're wallowing in, it doesn't make a difference where the fault lies. That's not important; it's just a distraction. How we clean it up is important. What's spilled can't be spilled again. You can't say, "Well, we need to figure out who did this so it won't happen again." It can't happen the same way again, anyway. Sometimes I don't understand anything about how it happened. And sometimes I think it's a combination of shifts in American culture: the dissolution of religion; the death of major figures like Kennedy and King; the selling of the concept of a generation gap, when the older people turned on the younger people and exploited them and their sexuality; the loss of a faith in romance as a form of engagement.

Anthony, we need healers. And I know what you're thinking: "I hear you, Wynton. But I'm just a musician in training." Remember what I told you weeks ago, when we set off down this road? We have to talk about music and life, because, ultimately, they end up as one and the same. Think of all that I've said and all that you've asked. Think of the notions floating in your own head—from integrity, to practice habits, to sifting information, to becoming your own teacher. Well, all of it, Ant, all of it tracks back to how you heal your culture one patient at a time, beginning with yourself. Antonioni, maybe your prairie won't be ten thousand square miles. But pick some real estate, man. And cover it. Hey, we got plenty of buckshot to go around. I'll see you back in New York.

Later when you straighter. (That's what Herlin always says.)

10

Dancing with Joy

September 28, 2003

Dear Anthony,

We spend so much time talking about problems, all these life philosophies roiling the brain. Even when we're practicing, we're still always thinking about what's wrong. We have to realize: What keeps you playing is what's right. You're not going to keep pursuing something that tastes nasty; it's got to have some sweetness somewhere in it. (Herlin says you can attract flies with honey as well as with shit.) And the thing about jazz, through all the business involved in practicing and improvement, it's always sweet: the improvement that you notice in the ability to express yourself, the feeling of playing, pushing yourself out into an open space through a sound, man. That's an unbelievable feeling, an uplifting feeling of joy to be able to express the range of what you feel and see, have felt and have seen. A lot of this has nothing to do with you. It comes from another time, another space. To be able to channel those things and then project them through an instrument, that's something that brings unbelievable joy.

You know, a musician's joy comes from a lot of sources: the people who come to hear you project your own joy in cities and towns; the bandmates, the brothers who project their joy right beside you; and all the other good people who help form the shape of the road—from the older musicians, to kids, to women. And you should seek these things and know them well, perhaps more than anything else.

When our band plays in towns across the country, people will sometimes stand in line for hours after the show to have us sign autographs or listen to their kids play. Makes me wonder: How do people in a small town like this even know who we are, what we do? It could be in a small town or even a nice-sized city like Sacramento, on a Wednesday night, sold-out concerts. I meet people bringing food, pies, and cookies and cooking meals for us all the time. Wanting us to taste this or that from their town. This music lifts people. You'll see things you'll never ever want to forget.

We played in Istanbul some years back. A few of us went out to the cymbal factory with Herlin Riley, our drummer. We were standing just outside the cymbal factory, just in the neighborhood, you know. A guy stood on the street eating; he saw we came from the United States. He wanted to come over, chat about religion, just congregate. Kids on the street started whispering about Michael Jackson, pointing at Herlin, 'cause all they knew was Michael Jackson at that time.

We were close to a housing project. A girl sat up on the balcony, she was maybe thirteen or fourteen. The people kept saying, "She speaks English, she's studying English in school." So she spoke a little broken English, talked to us. Then she disappeared. Dusk started to come on. After a moment, she reappeared, coming down to the street with some Turkish coffee for us in what had to be her family's best silverware. She poured it and stood there while we drank it. It was tender, man; had a sweetness to it. And that's the soulful thing about playing: You offer something to somebody. You don't know if they'll like it, but you offer it. Like she did.

And the cats, they're incredible, all of them. The people you spend all this time with will bring you great joy as well. Our rhythm section: Herlin Riley? He's from the Earth; bassist Carlos Henriquez, quick as lightning; our piano player, top Professor Eric Lewis. Unbridled creativity, man.

And our trombone players: Andre Hayward, with his big buttery sound, a sound that will heal your whole soul; the mercurial complexity of Ron Westray, a combination of sophistication and South Carolina country soul. I played a gig for Westray back in South Carolina. Man! The whole community turned out. I had never seen that for a musician from that area of the South. White people, black people, everybody. It was a big old thing.

Our sax players: Ted Nash and I came to New York around the same time. Both our fathers are musicians. He has two daughters who are around the age of my two oldest sons. The purity of his musicianship and his ability to relate to people for who they are—that is the thing we all love and respect about him. And Victor Goines, sweeping and swooping through the music. He and I played in our elementary school band together. We were eight years old, playing together, and now we are in our early forties, still swinging and playing together.

Playing with musicians is a gift. The thing that makes it so special is that they range so widely in age and the places they hail from. Like Joe Temperley, in his seventies: He probably has the most integrity in the band, man. Shows up first. Warms up. Gives me a call and says, "Send me my parts first." Joe has a lot of pride. He's the moral center of the band in many ways. We respect him because he embraced the music. He's from

Scotland. He didn't buy into any bullshit. He plays music; that's what he's about. You can't turn Joe around.

You gotta hope and work for that kind of fraternity, man. 'Cause you can't make it out here by yourself. I learned that from Marcus Roberts. You can't make it by yourself. Playing this music can be the most intimate thing you ever do with another man. You get so close to them, to their mind and what they're thinking, and you actually revel in every moment of it.

This is our life, man. And we revel in it. You'll find joy in other people, the people you meet. The older musicians, the younger ones, the tunes, people's sounds. The way people hold hands entering a concert. The way kids stand when playing their instruments, or parents when taking a picture.

You remember all your experiences. I remember kids who came to me for lessons, man, and they were nervous. Kids who would become great players in their own right. I remember Marcus Roberts after we played his first gig; he said, "Well, I played a gig now."

"Don't worry," I told him. "By the end of this year, man, we'll play so many gigs you won't remember the count."

Stories are what this music is about.

The great bass player Milt Hinton was real, real sick. One of our young teenage bassists, Carlos Henriquez, wanted to go see him. Carlos and I picked up Reginald Veal and Rodney Whitaker, two other phenomenal young bassists. We got lost going way out to Queens, but finally got there late. Milt's wife, Mona, said, "I don't know, you all might have come over too late. Milt can't get up, you know, he can't play." Man, when Milt saw us, he got up—got his basses out, and couldn't stop himself from playing. Milt was something, man. The fellas started playing with Milt. Got him off that bed. They started slapping those basses and just started crying. Got so full, he had to let it out. Well, Milt passed away right after that. He was ninety years old, man.

Mark O'Connor is a great American violinist, fiddler, and composer. One night our band went to some of his friends' house. His two sons, Forrest and Gage, were there, too. He pulled his fiddle out after we ate and started playing, and playing, and playing. He played a tune he had learned from his teachers when he was a boy. Man, you should have seen how *his* boys looked at him. Then he came and played with us at the gig the next night. The mike started falling, and he followed the microphone right down to the floor; he was playing so much, he didn't want to stop. That's how this music is, man.

Jon Hendricks, the legendary jazz vocalist, at eighty-something years old, drove two hours to get to a gig we did in Ohio. He sits in on our two-and-a-half-hour gig. Then we go to a jam session later that night. We're sitting up, looking at him, it's maybe three-thirty in the morning. And he's looking over to me: Let's play one more, man! That's what this music

is about. Let's play one more. He don't want it to ever stop.
And he got to drive two hours back home.

I think about the joy we gave to some musicians, to the
people who are not here anymore, like Milt, or Sweets Edison.
I'll be somewhere and somebody will give me a picture of us
with Sweets. And I think about the time that Sweets came to
one of our rehearsals of Basie's music. He's sitting back there
in the trumpet section, singing all the parts, telling stories
about different cats. Who wrote what. Who came home and
caught his ol' lady cheating. What words they used to sing
different phrases. He's making us feel like we are extensions of
the Basie band from the thirties. The 1930s!, man. The Great
Depression. Memories like that, memories of the music go on
and on and on.

Another time, I got to Ornette Coleman's house at about
11 P.M.; when we took our horns out of our mouths it was
4 A.M.! And I didn't want to leave.

Joy comes in the human experiences you have when
you're out there playing. A man and a woman. Oh, yes. You
can't hide from that; that's a part of it. It might be *all* of it.
Being on the road is a lonely thing. And music is a very romantic, sensual pursuit. Through it, you're always giving
shape to the invisible. There are ebbs and flows, rises and falls,
a lot of flirtation. You use a lot of sexual energy to play music.
And not just for slow songs. You use a lot of male energy *and*

female energy. Man, the sweetest gifts you'll get in your life will probably come from a woman. You know, it's not just a sexual thing. It's important because it becomes a part of the music and a part of your understanding of life and just how sweet something can be. Or how something can be sweet but have a bitter undertow. If you don't know about that, what you gonna play?

It's difficult for jazz musicians: the balance of family and the road. Yeah, it's almost impossible. If you work all the time, you have to make a choice. Or you have to reach an understanding with your old lady. It won't be easy. But you can't be great working part-time, that's not going to happen. We've all made that choice: no part-time music. That's a choice we wanted to make. A lot of other guys didn't make that decision. They stayed home.

It never felt like a trade-off to me. I knew I would sacrifice everything to do this. And I did. You know, I keep my kids with me out on the road. It's crazy for them. But when they look back, they're going to cherish the experience. I try to let them see the craziness of it all. I don't try to shield them. Having my kids here, the other guys' kids, that's a source of joy all by itself. 'Cause we grew up like that, too. Not on the road, necessarily, but our parents played music. That's part of our way of life. And the musicians don't coddle you. They are very matter-of-fact. And if you can't handle it—handle it (MF).

I love that my kids know the other musicians. The fact that my sons know men like Herlin Riley, or Wycliffe Gordon. The fact that when my son was young, he sat there with Joe Temperley, playing the bass clarinet. My son doesn't play the clarinet anymore, but I'm just glad that he knows men like Joe Temperley and Wes Anderson, men of soul and substance. And my boys don't have to be musicians themselves. This is hard, man. I want them to be whatever they choose. I always teach my boys that their life is their own. That's the best thing you can do for your kids when you're a parent. I take care of them because I want to take care of them. I don't love them in exchange for anything. That's one of the hardest lessons to learn about loving, and life in general.

I didn't understand this when I was younger. That's why I got so hurt when I felt like my brother sold me out, leaving to go off and play pop music. If that happened now, I would understand it from his point of view. Why shouldn't he do it? I've learned. You can't aspire for something for another person. If you love someone, that's it. You have to let him or her be. Love isn't a bargain or a barter. And it's hard, because so much of relationship etiquette seems based on the notion "If I do this, then you should do that." But people, whether your children, siblings, or friends, they got their own lives and their own aspirations. And so, with my own kids, I really go out of my way not to impose my expectations. Now, you have to put *some* expectations on your kids, for their grades and the like. But it's important to liberate them to be themselves, to let them pursue their own dance with joy.

Always pursue that joy, the sweetness. Don't work solely out of a negative frame of reference. I know some of the discussions we've had make it seem as though things are always presented that way: bullshit going on, corruption, people not doing their share of this work. Truth is, all of that is to help you identify a *positive* frame of reference. You should create out of a positive frame of reference; that will sustain you out here. Living is a positive experience. That's what the blues teaches you. That's why it continues to exist. And that's why it's in so much music. Yeah, all of this tragic stuff happened to you, but you're still here. And you can still express being here with style. Like laughing to keep from crying. And you keep dancing, man. With music, with jazz, it's all dancing. Just like that first real good slow dance you ever have, when you get to just rub all over against a girl and you can't believe it. You feel like you can crawl inside her. And you don't ever want it to stop. Ebbing and flowing, you're trying to become one. It's unpredictable, giddy, the feeling of coming together with somebody else. Immeasurable joy. And you're doing it in time. You better enjoy it. You better, because it's unrelivable. That's jazz.

Sweet dreams, man.

WYNTON MARSALIS, artistic director of Jazz at Lincoln Center, musician, educator, and composer, was born in New Orleans and received his first trumpet from renowned jazz musician Al Hirt at the age of six. Throughout his high school years, Marsalis studied jazz and classical trumpet with John Longo, Norman Smith, George Jansen, and Bill Fielder, and went on to study at the Juilliard School of Music. While in New York, he performed in the pit orchestra for Stephen Sondheim's *Sweeney Todd* on Broadway, and with the Brooklyn Philharmonic. He played with and learned from great older jazz musicians such as Clark Terry, Roy Eldridge, Harry "Sweets" Edison, and Dizzy Gillespie, and began playing regularly with master drummer Art Blakey, later joining Blakey's band, the Jazz Messengers, for a year and a half. To date, Marsalis has won nine Grammy awards, in both jazz and classical categories, and is the only artist to have won Grammy awards in five consecutive years, from 1983 to 1987. In 1997, Marsalis's oratorio on slavery and freedom, *Blood on the Fields*, became the first and only jazz composition to date to win the Pulitzer Prize in music.

SELWYN SEYFU HINDS is a noted author and award-winning journalist. He is the former editor in chief of *The Source* magazine and, more recently, executive editor of *Savoy* magazine. In 2002 Mr. Hinds penned the critically hailed memoir *Gunshots in My Cook-Up*. His articles and criticisms have appeared in a range of publications, including *Vanity Fair, Spin, Vibe, USA Weekend*, and *The Village Voice*, where he began his writing career. A graduate of Princeton University, Hinds lives in Brooklyn, New York.

This book is set in Fournier, a typeface named for
Pierre Simon Fournier, the youngest son of a
French printing family. He started out engraving
woodblocks and large capitals, then moved on to
fonts of type. In 1736 he began his own foundry
and made several important contributions in the
field of type design; he is said to have cut 147
alphabets of his own creation. Fournier is probably
best remembered as the designer of St. Augustine
Ordinaire, a face that served as the model for
Monotype's Fournier, which was released in 1925.